# Reading Retardation and Multi-Sensory Teaching

# International Library of Psychology

General editor: Max Coltheart
*Professor of Psychology, University of London*

# Reading Retardation and Multi-Sensory Teaching

**Charles Hulme**
Department of Psychology
University of York

**Routledge & Kegan Paul**
London, Boston and Henley

First published in 1981
by Routledge & Kegan Paul Ltd
39 Store Street,
London WC1E 7DD,
9 Park Street,
Boston, Mass. 02108, USA and
Broadway House,
Newtown Road,
Henley-on-Thames,
Oxon RG9 1EN
Printed in Great Britain by
Redwood Burn Limited, Trowbridge & Esher

British Library Cataloguing in Publication Data

Hulme, Charles
Reading retardation and multi-sensory teaching.
(International library of psychology)
1.   Reading—Remedial teaching
I.   Title      II.   Series
371.92   LB1050.5

ISBN 0-7100-0761-2

For my parents

# Contents

# Figures

# Acknowledgments

This book is based on my doctoral thesis and the research reported here was carried out at the Department of Experimental Psychology, University of Oxford. I owe a great intellectual debt to my thesis supervisors, Dr Donald Broadbent and Dr Peter Bryant. Both helped me enormously during all stages of this research; not least by reading the whole of an earlier draft of this work. Their perceptive comments have greatly improved the finished product and it is a pleasure to acknowledge their help. Needless to say, any errors which remain are entirely my own responsibility.

Dr Lynette Bradley was also a great help to me in carrying out this research. She generously shared her extensive knowledge of children's reading problems and remedial teaching with me and provided the reading ages and IQs of the children seen in Experiment 3. I should also like to thank the staff and pupils of the schools who made this research possible; several teachers were more than generous in their co-operation.

Finally, my wife Jeanetta has been a constant source of help and encouragement. She quickly and efficiently typed various drafts of the manuscript and helped in checking the references and proofreading.

The Social Science Research Council provided financial support in the form of a Graduate Studentship.

# 1 The nature and causes of reading retardation

INTRODUCTION

Reading is arguably the most complex skill generally taught
in our culture, and failure in learning to read is clearly
highly detrimental educationally and socially.   Problems in
reading are relatively recent.   It is only in the past century
and a quarter that mass literacy has come to western
Europe;  where between 1850 and 1950 the rate of literacy
has risen from 50-5 per cent to 92 per cent of the adult
population (Cipolla, 1969).   With this rise in literacy,
pressures on individuals to be literate have increased and
official concern is expressed from time to time about the
standards of reading in this country (e.g. Bullock, 1975).
   It is now generally recognised that there are a number of
children of adequate general intelligence who nevertheless
experience inordinate difficulties in learning to read.   This
book examines some of the possible reasons for these
children's reading difficulties, and at the same time explores
the basis of a teaching technique which is reputed to help
them learn to read.   We begin with the historical background
to these ideas.

HISTORY

In 1895 James Hinshelwood, a Glasgow eye surgeon,
described the case of a 58-year-old teacher who suddenly,
apparently as the result of a stroke, lost the ability to read.
Although he could see adequately he was unable to name
letters or to read simple words.   Hinshelwood named this
inability 'word blindness' and attributed it to a loss of visual

1

memory for words. He considered the disorder was related to visual agnosia (mind blindness in his terminology); both being disturbances of visual memory for different classes of stimuli. He envisaged memory for these different stimuli to depend on distinct systems which could be selectively impaired by lesions of different brain regions. To quote from a later publication:

> It has been the endeavour of the author to show that letter, word and mind-blindness in all the varieties met with in clinical experience can be intelligibly explained by regarding them as disorders of the visual memory, produced by lesions affecting more or less completely a definite area of the cerebral cortex in which are preserved these past visual impressions arranged in definite and ordered groups. (Hinshelwood, 1900)

Prompted by Hinshelwood's original article, Morgan (1896) wrote of the case of a 14-year-old boy who, although of very good intelligence, had a profound inability to learn to read. Morgan considered this to represent a case of 'congenital word blindness' which he thought may have been caused by the faulty development of the left angular gyrus, the brain region implicated in adult cases of word blindness. Following Hinshelwood, Morgan attributed the boy's difficulties to an inability to store the visual impressions of words.

These two reports had a profound effect on subsequent developments. Hinshelwood continued to study cases of reading problems in adults and children culminating in his two monographs 'Letter-, Word- and Mind-Blindness' (1900), and 'Congenital Word-Blindness' (1917). Cases, such as the one Morgan had reported, of children with marked reading difficulties were consistently interpreted as comparable to the adult cases and as problems of visual memory. To quote Hinshelwood (1917) once more:

> The defect in these children is then a strictly specialised one viz. a difficulty in acquiring and storing up in the brain the visual memories of words and letters.

This emphasis on visual factors as an explanation for reading problems was particularly significant. Reading, superficially at least, appears to be a predominantly visual skill, and so it seems natural that cases of reading difficulties should be referred to an eye specialist such as Hinshelwood. In addition, Hinshelwood's training was almost certainly responsible for his emphatic explanation in terms of deficient visual memory. In his case reports, however, there seems to have been no compelling reason for explana-

tions in terms of visual rather than verbal memory.  He
does not seem to have considered this alternative, however.

The other major figure in the history of reading difficulties who must be mentioned is an American neurologist,
Samuel T. Orton.  His influential work with children was
reported in his book 'Reading, Writing and Speech Problems
in Children' (1937).  Orton was clearly influenced by
Hinshelwood and, like him, viewed reading problems as
deficits of visual memory, which were best understood in
relation to studies of adults with reading problems stemming
from brain lesions.  Orton modified earlier conceptions in
several ways, however.  While agreeing with Hinshelwood's
view that the parallels between reading impairments seen in
brain damaged adults and those seen in some children
implied a common physiological mechanism, he thought that
childhood cases probably reflected continuous variations in
performance within the population rather than any definite
lesion.  He was also intensely interested in brain laterality
and was struck by an apparent excess of children with reading difficulties who showed evidence of poorly developed
cerebral dominance in tests of hand, eye and foot preference.
He inferred from this that it was likely that these children's
brains were also incompletely lateralised for language functions.  He tried to unite these ideas with a further observation that these children made many reversals in their reading
and spelling, confusing letters such as 'b' and 'd' which
differed only in their orientation, and making similar mis-
takes with words, such as confusing 'was' and 'saw'.  He
attributed these reversals to the existence of mirror image
engrams in the two hemispheres of these poorly lateralised
children.  Normally, he argued, the engrams underlying the
visual memory of words, were only firmly established in the
hemisphere dominant for language.  Orton's stress on the
prevalence of reversals in the reading and spelling errors
of these children led him to propose the term 'strephosymbolia' (literally, twisted symbols) for their condition.

There seems to be an outstanding logical problem with
these early conceptions of reading problems as deficits of
visual memory.  Both Hinshelwood and Orton clearly state,
as their clinical experience apparently forced them to, that
the proposed deficit in visual memory was completely restricted to verbal materials.  They do not, however, specify
any characteristic of written language which differentiated
it from other classes of stimuli and resulted in it being
uniquely represented in a distinct brain structure.

Hinshelwood's early cases demonstrated that patients could lose the ability to read letters and words independently of each other, and also that some patients with a complete inability to read letters and words could still read Arabic numerals. It seems hard to envisage a system which would categorise these physically highly similar stimuli into distinct categories whose visual representations were segregated.

Evidence relevant to these conceptions of reading problems will be dealt with later. For present purposes, it can simply be stated that, from the beginning a clear emphasis on visual memory disturbances as a cause of reading problems was evident, and this emphasis, although not well founded logically or empirically, has continued to the present day.


## PREVALENCE AND TERMINOLOGY

The early reports of reading problems came from the medical profession and were couched in neurological language. The term 'dyslexia' was originally applied to adults who had lost the ability to read following brain injury. It was later applied to cases of children who had severe reading problems, because early reports had stressed the similarities between them and the adult cases. Educationalists have taken exception to this medical concept of reading problems in children on two counts. It has been disputed that the term 'dyslexia' with its neurological connotations accurately described a group of children with reading difficulties and, more radically, whether there even exists a significant group of children whose constitutional make-up hampers their learning to read (e.g. Morris, 1966).

There are at least two questions here. First, whether there are a significant number of children who in the absence of any general intellectual impairment have a marked difficulty learning to read. Second, if such children exist, whether the description implied by the term dyslexia is an accurate one.

(a) Prevalence. To answer this first question we must look to population surveys of children's reading ability. By far the most extensive and methodologically satisfactory survey of this type is that of the Maudsley group (Rutter, Tizard and Whitmore, 1970) which screened the entire population of 9-, 10- and 11-year-olds resident on the Isle of Wight. Most attention will be given to this study and its findings, others being mentioned by way of comparison to it.

In considering the incidence of reading difficulties it is necessary to define criteria for expected achievement and set cut-off points in relation to this, below which children are classified as having significant difficulty. In the work of Rutter et al. (1970), an important distinction is drawn between reading backwardness and reading retardation. Backwardness describes reading which is backward in relation to the child's age regardless of intelligence. Retardation is a more precise term referring to a specific difficulty in learning to read, specific in the sense that it is not explicable in terms of the child's general intelligence. Clearly, if one is interested in factors specific to reading it is necessary to control for IQ. Retardation is defined in terms of multiple regression formulae in which expected reading level is predicted on the basis of a known relationship between reading, IQ and age in the total population. In the Isle of Wight study retardation was defined as an attainment on reading accuracy or comprehension 2 years 4 months below that expected on the basis of age and IQ. Backwardness in contrast was defined simply as an attainment of 2 years 4 months below age norms. Intelligence was measured using a short form of the Wechsler Intelligence Scale for Children (WISC), reading with a prose reading test, the Neale Analysis of Reading Ability.

Using these definitions which are clearly quite stringent, reading retardation and backwardness had incidence rates of 3.7 per cent and 6.6 per cent respectively amongst 9-11-year-olds on the Isle of Wight. These figures were considered to be slight underestimates due to imperfections in screening. In a follow-up study, two years later, the same population was again screened and a further $\frac{1}{2}$ per cent of children were found to be retarded who had not been detected in the initial study. Thus, in an area considered similar in terms of social composition to the rest of England as a whole, a conservative estimate is that as many as 4 per cent of the children have severe and specific difficulties in learning to read.

The same group of workers also studied reading attainment in an Inner London borough and found that reading problems there were much more common than in the Isle of Wight (Berger, Yule and Rutter, 1975). Using the same procedure and criteria as in the Isle of Wight study, specific reading retardation was found to occur in 9.9 per cent of 10-year-olds and reading backwardness in 19 per cent of these

children.  This was after immigrant children, who may be
expected to have difficulties learning to read because of
language problems, had been excluded.  Thus, in this inner
city area, reading problems were nearly three times as
common as in the Isle of Wight, an area considered socially
representative of the country as a whole.  Such differences
between populations are difficult to interpret.  Rutter,
Yule, Quinton, Rowlands, Yule and Berger (1975) suggest
several environmental factors which may account for the
differences in the rates of educational and psychiatric
problems they found in the children of these two areas.
Adverse social factors such as marital difficulties, psychiatric disorder in the parents, larger family size and cramped
living conditions;  and adverse school conditions such as
high proportions of immigrant children, high rates of absen-
teeism and high rates of staff turnover, were both more
common in the London borough.

Differences in the criteria used to define reading backwardness and retardation and differences in the age groups
studied makes direct comparison with other survey data
impossible.  The most that can be said is that other data do
not seriously conflict with these estimates.

Clark (1970) carried out a survey in which all Dumbarton-
shire children were screened at 7 years of age;  of these
15 per cent had hardly started to read and were followed up
for intensive study at age 9 years when the WISC and Neale
Analysis of Reading Ability were used.  The 9-year-olds
with signs of reading difficulty who were intensively studied
were selected to be of average IQ which was defined by a
verbal or performance IQ of 90 or above.  Within this
group, a subgroup equivalent to 1.2 per cent of the population were 2 years or more retarded for age in reading, and
the equivalent of 5.1 per cent of the population were from 1
to 2 years retarded for age.  No check on the reliability of
screening was carried out by Clark, so that these figures
again are probably underestimates.  Even allowing for
this, however, the figure of 1.2 per cent for children 2
years or more retarded in reading does seem low in comparison to the Isle of Wight figure of 4 per cent of children 2
years 4 months or more retarded.  The use of regression
techniques to equate for IQ and the older sample in the Isle
of Wight study would both lead to higher estimates of the
number of reading retardates in a given sample.  Conversely, Clark's criteria of 2 years below norms was more
lenient than the Isle of Wight criteria of 2 years 4 months.

It is of course impossible to say, given present evidence, how these various factors may work out numerically.

Two other studies which have only considered backward-ness may be briefly mentioned. Pringle, Butler and Davie (1966), in a National Federation for Educational Research sponsored, national survey of 7-year-olds found that 10 per cent had barely made a start with reading. Morris (1966) in a large study of Kent schoolchildren found that amongst 8-year-olds 14 per cent were reading not at all, or very poorly, and 7 per cent continued having difficulty throughout school.

In conclusion, whatever figures one chooses to emphasise it is clear that reading difficulties are a sizeable problem in the community at large. The best figures we have suggest that as many as four children in every hundred experience a specific difficulty in learning to read which is independent of general intelligence as measured by IQ tests.

(b) The normality of the distribution of reading scores and the validity of the concept of specific reading retarda-tion. These questions have only been explicitly considered by the Maudsley group (reviewed by Rutter and Yule, 1975). Yule, Rutter, Berger and Thompson (1974) showed that in five population studies (four sub-populations in the Isle of Wight study and one survey in London) the rate of severe specific reading retardation defined by regression techniques in all cases exceeded that predicted on the assumption that reading ability is a normally distributed variable. There was no equivalent excess of over-achievers.

The question arises as to whether this 'hump' in the dis-tribution of reading achievement represents the existence of a distinct group of children with specific difficulties, analo-gous to the mental defectives who represent a comparable 'hump' on the IQ distribution. Evidence for this possibility comes from an examination of the correlates of reading back-wardness and reading retardation (Rutter et al., 1970; Rutter and Yule, 1975). First, the sex distribution in these two groups was quite different. In the backward readers 54 per cent were boys while in the retarded readers 77 per cent were boys; expressed as sex ratios these figures are 1.3 to 1 and 3.3 to 1 respectively. Neurological examina-tions also revealed differences; overt brain dysfunction and dubious neurological signs were both far more common in the backward group than the retarded. This same picture was also reflected in tests for motor and praxic abnormalities both of which were significantly more common in the backward

than in the retarded readers.  Family histories and interviews were used to assess speech and language functions
and both groups were impaired to a similar degree on these
measures.  For example, both groups showed evidence of
slow speech development and commonly had family histories
of reading and speech difficulties.  The backward readers
did differ from retarded readers, however, in showing
significantly lower complexity of language as assessed at
interview.  Perhaps the most striking feature differentiating the two groups was their educational prognosis which was
assessed in a follow-up study four to five years later when
they were $14\frac{1}{2}$ years old (Yule, 1973).  At this time they
were given the Neale Analysis of Reading Ability, the
Schonell spelling test and the Vernon arithmetic-maths test.
Despite their higher IQ the retarded readers had made significantly less progress in reading and spelling than the
backward readers but more progress in arithmetic.

These findings taken together support the distinction
drawn between specific reading retardation and reading
backwardness.  Roughly speaking the latter emerge as a
group of low general ability which seems related to a high
incidence of signs indicative of minimal brain dysfunction.
The former group on the other hand experience more specific difficulties in learning to read which are associated with
a fairly specific language deficit in the absence of any
general intellectual impairment or frequent signs of brain
damage.  This is not to say, however, that these children
necessarily form an homogenous aetiological group.

(c) Terminology.  It is evident that there are a significant number of children who, despite adequate general
intelligence, encounter severe problems in learning to read.
The question remains whether they should be referred to as
dyslexic.  To an extent terminology is arbitrary and need
not concern us too much.  Use of the term 'dyslexia',
though poorly defined, implies the existence of a well
defined unitary condition when it is certainly not yet established that retarded readers form such a group.  In addition, it carries further implications about causation and the
neurological basis of these children's reading problems which
again are less than well substantiated.  Perhaps most
importantly, the symptoms associated with dyslexia, although
common amongst the retarded readers in the Isle of Wight
survey, did not cluster together.  Different children showed
different sub-grouping of these symptoms.  Furthermore,
selection of those children showing most 'dyslexic' symptoms

did not predict subsequent reading performance (Rutter, 1969).

For these reasons the term 'retarded readers' will be used to refer to children who for no apparently adequate reason fail to learn to read normally. If slightly inelegant, at least this term has the advantage of not pre-judging the nature and causes of these children's reading problems.


GENERAL FACTORS

When there are consistent individual differences in a certain type of behaviour, three broad types of causes for these differences are often distinguished. They may be innate, there may be biological factors in the environment which differentially affect individuals, and there may be influences in the psychological and social environment which determine these differences. The complexity of differentiating between these broad alternatives is well illustrated by the heated debates concerning the development of sex differences (Maccoby and Jacklin, 1975) and differences in IQ between groups (e.g. Kamin, 1974). Studies of reading retardation have also been concerned to distinguish between these broad classes of explanation. Though much of the evidence lacks precision, it seems likely that genetic, biological and social influences all play a role in the causation of reading retardation.


Genetics

From the earliest reports of children with severe reading retardation strong claims have been made about the genetic basis of the disorder. As early as 1905, Thomas and Fisher independently noted multiple cases in individual families. Hinshelwood (1917) and Orton (1937) also reported a strong tendency for the condition to run in families and interpreted this as a genetic effect. This emphasis has continued to the present day and 'constitutional origin' forms part of the definition of 'specific developmental dyslexia' adopted by the World Federation of Neurology (Critchley, 1970).

Although some evidence points to the operation of genetic influences none is conclusive. The first comes from family studies. Hallgren (1950) selected 116 Swedish children with reading problems and found that 88 per cent of these had at least one first degree relative with similar reading problems.  This study embodies serious methodological faults, however; in particular no criteria are given for diagnosing reading problems and in some cases, for example, deceased relatives were diagnosed on the basis of interviews with other family members.  In addition, no control group was included in the study.  The reliability of the findings is thrown into doubt by the fact that amongst the relatives, the incidence of reading problems showed no sex bias, which conflicts with the almost universal finding of a bias of 3 or 4 to 1 in favour of males amongst retarded readers (Rutter and Yule, 1973).

Two better conducted family studies are available. Doehring (1968) reported that in a matched group of 37 retarded readers and 38 controls, reading problems were much more common amongst the families of the retarded readers. Of the parents of the retarded readers approximately 40 per cent reported reading problems compared to 10 per cent of the controls.  Likewise, there were over three times as many families of the retarded readers in which one or more individuals reported reading problems.  In the Isle of Wight study (Rutter et al., 1970) 34 per cent of the retarded readers compared to 9 per cent of controls had parents or siblings with reading problems.  In both these studies, however, it is not possible to say whether the reading problems of the relatives were specific or a symptom of more general educational problems.  Furthermore, even if such evidence was available, data from family studies can be interpreted in terms of social rather than genetic influences.

Some twin studies have also been interpreted as evidence for the importance of genetic factors.  Monozygotic (MZ) twins develop from the same fertilised ovum and so are genetically more similar than dizygotic (DZ) twin pairs, who, genetically, are only as similar as any other pair of siblings.  The extent to which MZ twins are more similar to each other on a given characteristic than are DZ twins is often interpreted as evidence for a genetic influence on the development of that characteristic.  This interpretation depends on the assumption that the environments of the MZ twins are no more similar to each other than those of the DZ twins.  As in the case of other complex behaviours we are fairly ignorant of any critical environmental factors which may influence the development of reading retardation.  On present knowledge, however, the assumption of MZ twins having equally similar environments to DZ twins seems a reasonable one.

The few twin studies that have considered reading retardation have reported higher concordance rates for MZ than DZ twins. Hermann (1959) found 100 per cent concordance in 12 MZ twin pairs compared to 33 per cent in 33 DZ pairs. Similarly, Bakwin(1973) found 84 per cent concordance in 31 MZ pairs compared with 29 per cent in 31 DZ pairs. Both these studies suffer from the same methodological error of giving no criteria for the diagnosis of reading retardation. As reading difficulties are common, there can be no confidence in reports which lack an exact specification of the criteria of diagnosis.

These twin studies, like the family studies, are at best suggestive evidence of a genetic influence on reading retardation. Even if better conducted twin studies presented the same pattern of results the exact nature of any genetic factor would remain unclear. Since there is some evidence for a genetic determinant of reading ability in the general population (Jensen, 1969) this could account for such a pattern of results and it would remain unclear whether there was a more specific factor operating in cases of reading retardation.

In conclusion, a genetic factor in at least some cases of reading retardation remains likely if unproven. To a degree, the extent to which genetic factors are responsible for these children's problems is not of great practical importance. It may be better to concentrate on understanding the nature of the disorder so that we are better able to teach them to read.

Environmental influences

If we know little about the genetics of reading retardation we probably know even less about the more complex question of specific environmental influences. Reading is, above all, a skill which is taught. Even if, as seems likely, there are genetic influences operating in cases of reading retardation, it is obvious that teaching must affect the development of these children's difficulties. As mentioned earlier adverse school conditions were correlated with the higher rates of reading problems in an Inner London borough as compared to the Isle of Wight (Rutter et al., 1975). Such correlations must be treated cautiously, however, given the complexity of the differences between different areas. It would be more satisfying if with the use of specific teaching methods retarded readers could be taught to read. One might then be able to see if schools which ignored certain teaching methods produced more retarded readers. Such evidence is not available, however. Yule (1976) and Carroll (1972) have reviewed studies of the remedial teaching of reading and both conclude there is little evidence for its effectiveness. Clearly, such a conclusion must be interpreted cautiously. Inadequacies in the studies such as the short duration of the remedial teaching and the use of teachers without specific training, render these failures less than compelling.

It remains true that evidence linking specific variables in the school environment to the occurrence of reading retardation appears to be lacking. The idea that poor teaching exacerbates the problems of children who experience specific difficulties in learning to read remains very plausible and deserves further study. Furthermore, the lack of evidence for the effectiveness of remedial teaching underlines the desirability of increasing our understanding of specific remedial teaching procedures, by experimental studies such as those reported in later chapters.

Studies of school conditions remain the most likely way of demonstrating the influence of environmental variables on reading retardation. Longitudinal studies would appear feasible and highly desirable in this area. The influence of the home environment has also been studied, but here any effects seem likely to be more diffuse. There is evidence that family size influences reading attainment. In the Isle of Wight study there was a strong association between large family size and reading retardation (Rutter et al., 1970). Of the retarded readers 58 per cent came from families with four or more children, compared with only 33 per cent of controls. Other studies, which have only considered attainment independently of IQ, give the same picture. Morris (1966), in Kent, found that 22 per cent of poor readers had more than three siblings compared to 5 per cent of good readers. This association of large family size with reading attainment seems to be part of a more general association between family size and verbal ability. Douglas (1964) in a large national sample found that large family size was associated with low scores on vocabulary and reading tests but less so with tests of non-verbal intelligence. In the National Child Development Study (Davie, Butler and

Goldstein, 1972) large family size was related to reading attainment but only slightly to arithmetic.  Similarly, Nisbet and Entwistle (1967) found that there was a greater association between family size and verbal than non-verbal ability.

It seems likely that children in large families receive less verbal stimulation from adults and spend more time in the company of young children who are less verbally stimulating. This is supported by the finding that the effects of large family size on verbal ability are increased by the presence of younger children in the home (Nisbet, 1953;  Douglas, Ross and Simpson, 1968;  Davie et al., 1972).  It is likely then that being in a large family has an adverse effect on language development and this later influences reading development.

Other variables of home life that have been studied with regard to reading attainment are the availability of reading materials in the home, and parental attitudes to their children's reading.  Both these correlate with reading attainment (Davie et al., 1972;  Morris, 1966) but their importance in cases of reading retardation remains unknown.


Biological factors

The idea that reading retardation depends on some subtle impairment of brain function is another persistent idea dating from the early studies by neurologists.  In looking at the evidence for this claim, problems of sampling are acute (Rutter et al., 1970).  It is clearly unlikely that those retarded readers referred to neurologists will constitute an unbiased sample.  Because of this it would be easy to arrive at a distorted view of the prevalence of neurological complications in these children based on studies of referrals to neurological clinics.  The question is not whether any children retarded in reading have minor neurological deficits.  Rather it is how important such deficits are as a possible cause of the reading problems of this large and possibly heterogeneous group.  For this reason most emphasis will be given to the findings of the Isle of Wight study (Rutter et al., 1970) as this appears to be the only population survey to have looked at the neurological status of retarded readers.

The findings of this survey have already been briefly referred to in relation to the distinction between reading

retardation and reading backwardness (pp. 7-8).
Each child selected for intensive study was given a full
neurological examination. Of the 86 retarded readers in
the sample none had a definite neurological abnormality, and
although the rate of 'possible' abnormalities was higher in
the retarded readers (18.6 per cent) than in the controls
(13 per cent), the difference was not statistically significant. On the other hand, 18 per cent of epileptic children
and 40 per cent of children with cerebral palsy and other
brain conditions in this study were retarded in their reading.
This apparent paradox reflects the rarity of these latter
conditions in comparison to reading retardation and also the
fact that cerebral palsy tends to be associated with general
intellectual impairment which precludes a diagnosis of reading retardation. So although reading retardation may be
caused by overt brain damage this only accounts for a very
small proportion of observed cases.

The incidence of minor or soft neurological signs was
much higher, however, in the retarded readers than in the
controls. These are tests of age related functions as
opposed to the tests for overt abnormalities referred to
above. So, for example, spasticity is abnormal at any age,
while motor co-ordination is something which develops
gradually and for which age-related norms exist. Motor
development (as assessed by parental reports of the age at
which milestones such as sitting, walking and bowel control
were achieved) was slowed in the retarded readers and they
showed greater clumsiness in tests of fine and gross movements. They also showed signs of motor impersistence on
a test where the child is required to sustain certain volun-
tary motor acts initiated by verbal commands. Although it
is ill-understood, this test is performed poorly by brain
damaged children (Garfield, 1964). The retarded readers
were also poor on constructional tests requiring the copying
of geometric designs with matches. Speech and language
were assessed by parental reports of past developments and
in a structured interview with the child. The retarded
readers were significantly worse on both these types of
measures. Finally, although laterality tests did not differentiate the retarded readers from controls, they did show
confusion between right and left more often than controls.
A reasonable conclusion, therefore, is that although very
few retarded readers show signs of definite brain damage,
the development of their nervous systems probably lags
behind that of normal children.

One possible explanation for these minor neurological
signs in retarded readers would be in terms of genetics.
As we have seen, however, evidence for the operation of
genetic factors in the causation of this syndrome is weak at
best.   A more plausible explanation is in terms of pre- and
perinatal complications.   Kawi and Pasamanick (1958,
1959) compared the hospital birth records of a group of 205
boys with reading problems and a group of controls born in
the same area to mothers of the same age.   Of the children
with reading difficulties, 16.6 per cent had been exposed to
two or more maternal complications compared to 1.5 per cent
of the controls, and those complications most likely to cause
foetal anoxia were the most strongly implicated.   They also
found there were more premature births amongst the poor
readers (11.5 per cent) than the controls (4.6 per cent).
There are problems in interpreting these findings, however.
The groups of children were not matched for IQ so that any
differences in reading may have been partly non-specific.
Furthermore, the controls came from smaller families of
higher socio-economic status and these differences may also
have played a part in creating the differences in reading
attainment.

In the Isle of Wight study (Rutter et al., 1970) large
family size was correlated with poor reading attainment.
In that study complications of pregnancy were also examined
but by means of parental report which may limit the reliability of the findings.   A higher proportion of the retarded
readers were found to be premature, of low birth weight and
small in relation to gestational age, but none of these differences was statistically significant.   Lyle (1970) in a ques-
tionnaire study of mothers found no relation between reported perinatal factors and reading retardation.   The sample
here was smaller, however, and highly selected with regard
to social class variables, and again questionnaires of this
sort may not be reliable.

In conclusion it appears that although overt brain damage
can cause reading retardation, most children retarded in
reading do not show any definite neurological symptoms.
Signs of delayed brain development are common amongst
these children, however, and a possible explanation for this
is in terms of pre- and perinatal complications.

PSYCHOLOGICAL FACTORS

In considering the psychological mechanisms responsible
for reading retardation three broad approaches can be dis-
cerned.   First is the view that visual perceptual or memory
deficits are responsible.   A second approach is that there
may be a specific deficiency in the integration of visual and
auditory information, such as is required in learning to
read.   A third approach has looked for evidence of auditory
perceptual and general language impairments as causes of
reading difficulties.   Each of these approaches will be
considered in turn.   Before discussing detailed findings
some comments on methodology are appropriate.

Methodology

The typical experimental design in this area is to compare
the performance of a group of retarded readers and a group
of normal readers on a task thought to involve skills relevant
to learning to read.   As reading is the variable of interest
it is essential to match the groups for general intelligence.
Failure to do this renders some studies uninterpretable
because any difference found between such groups may as
easily be a function of intelligence as of reading ability.
Many studies do control for IQ, but even here any deficits
found amongst the retarded readers may not be easy to
interpret.   Most commonly such deficits have been interpreted as causes of the retarded readers difficulties.
    Such conclusions are unwarranted.   All that has been
shown in such a case is that the two groups differ in their
performance on some task.   Effectively this is a correlation between performance on the task and reading ability.
Low reading ability being associated with poor performance,
high reading ability with better performance.   Conclusions
about causes cannot be made from correlational evidence
alone.
    Logically there are three possible explanations for corre-
lations of this sort.   It may be, as commonly suggested,
that a task that is performed badly by retarded readers taps
a cause of their reading difficulty.   Alternatively, the
causal connection could be of the opposite form; their poor
performance on a task could be a consequence of not having
learned to read.   A third possibility is that some deficits
may be irrelevant to the retarded readers' difficulties.   An

example of this might be the delays shown amongst retarded readers in various motor functions described earlier.  Such delays are in themselves unlikely to cause reading problems. On the other hand, reading problems may depend on some general delay in the maturation of the CNS which is indexed by these abnormalities of motor development.  This particular line of reasoning is probably of great importance.  Given the evidence reviewed earlier that retarded readers may be characterised by some general immaturity of the CNS, it seems likely that their performance on many psychological tasks will deviate from that of normal children, but many of these deviations may be quite irrelevant to the cause of their reading problems.  The magnitude of this correlational problem has been greatly neglected in most studies to date.

There would seem to be three ways of reducing the ambiguities of such correlational findings.  First, one may add a further control group matched for reading achievement and IQ but whose reading is age appropriate, i.e., a younger control group (e.g. Bradley and Bryant, 1978).  This is the strategy adopted in chapter 3.  If the retarded readers are inferior on a given measure in comparison to such a group this difference cannot be attributed to their lack of reading experience or ability.  The probability of it being related to the cause of the reading problem is therefore increased. Some studies of the spelling patterns of retarded readers have made use of this type of comparison in the past (Frank, 1936; Orton, 1937; Tordrup, 1966), but paradoxically its advantages have not been appreciated until recently in studies of reading retardation.

The value of this type of comparison, between groups matched for reading age and IQ but differing in chronological age depends on the kind of results obtained.  These comparisons involve pitting the effects of an inferred deficit amongst the retarded readers against that of developmental trends in the processes of interest, e.g. various aspects of language development.  Negative results will be hard to interpret.  Failure to demonstrate a difference on a task between such groups when there was a difference between groups matched for age and IQ but differing in reading age, does not show that this difference was due to differences in reading experience or skill.  The difference may reflect a developmental lag in some process which does contribute to the retarded readers' difficulties.  On the other hand, positive results in such comparisons are important, as they may tell us something about the causes of reading retardation.

The logic behind this type of comparison is in fact exactly the same as in longitudinal studies. In these studies measurements of certain abilities are made in children before they have started to learn to read. Their progress in reading is then followed and related to these early measurements. If these measures are predictive of later reading failure at least one can be sure that this does not depend upon the effects of failure in reading. One advantage of studies which match on reading age is that they are easier to conduct than longitudinal studies. On the other hand, longitudinal studies are probably more likely to produce positive results, because they do not involve comparisons of groups of different ages.

The results of longitudinal studies or those in which subjects are matched for reading age still have a major problem of interpretation. This is that any deficits found which relate to reading retardation may be irrelevant to its cause. Interpretations here will be guided by the logical relationship between the task and the situation of learning to read. A causal interpretation in such a case can be strengthened by the second approach which is to forge explicit links between the observed deficit and the retarded readers' difficulties. This involves looking for evidence in the pattern of reading and writing errors made by these children which implicate the same type of difficulty. For example, if it could be shown that some retarded readers have poor visual memories the causal status of this finding might be supported by showing that their spelling errors tended to be visually dissimilar to the correct form of the word, but similar phonetically (cf Boder, 1973).

The third and most direct (and also the most difficult) way out of this correlational problem is to perform training studies aimed at correcting the inferred deficit and observe the effects of this on reading. Such studies, if positive, also require careful controls to separate the specific and non-specific influences which may operate in such situations. (A comparison may be made here with the problems involved in demonstrating the effectiveness of psychotherapy.) Although difficult to conduct, studies of this type probably provide the most direct route for demonstrating the causes of reading retardation. Given the imperfections in our basic knowledge in this area it is quite natural that there have been few studies of this type to date. Hopefully, as knowledge of the correlates of reading retardation improves, they will become increasingly common.

One or many types of reading retardation?

One other criticism of the many experimental studies of
reading retardation, which is not inherent in their design,
is the implication which they often carry that it is an homogenous syndrome. Reading is a highly complex skill and it
is clear that a variety of cognitive and perceptual difficulties might hamper its acquisition. Clinical reports have
often claimed that there may be distinct aetiological sub-
groups of retarded readers. Cotterell (1970a) and Vernon
(1970) have both claimed that there may be a group who
suffer primarily from a visual problem and another whose
primary difficulty is auditory or linguistic. Perhaps the
most well developed of these clinical classifications is that
of Boder (1973). She studied the reading and spelling
patterns of these children and concluded that three groups
could be identified; 'dysphonetic dyslexia' in which there is
an inability to develop phonetic word analysis and synthesis
skills; 'dyseidetic dyslexia' in which there is a visual problem which hampers the recognition of words as gestalts;
and a third group of mixed cases who display both types of
deficit.
    Attempts to delineate possible sub-groups statistically in
unselected samples of retarded readers have not been very
successful. Naidoo (1972) in a large sample of dyslexic
boys collected data on family history, neurological status,
and from a battery of psychological tests. The data were
subjected to cluster analysis, but readily interpretable
groups did not emerge. In so far as interest is centred on
a classification according to the underlying psychological
deficit, data from neurological tests and family history may
be inappropriate. Doehring and Hoshko (1977) also found a
complex pattern of results in a study of reading retarded and
a more heterogeneous group of learning disabled children.
Inclusion of the latter group and the use of test materials
with poorly understood characteristics may have been responsible for this. In a study of the psychological test profiles of retarded readers referred for neurological assessment, Mattis, French and Rapin (1975) suggested that there
may be three distinct syndromes: a language disorder group,
an articulation and grapho-motor dysco-ordination group
(motor difficulties in speech and copying) and a group with
visuo-perceptual problems. The first two groups accounted
for 76 per cent of the sample and the visuo-perceptual group
for 16 per cent.

Another approach to this problem has relied primarily on verbal/performance discrepancies on the WISC. Ingram and Reid (1956) originally suggested that retarded readers whose scores on performance sub-tests were significantly lower than on verbal sub-tests tended to show errors of a visuo-spatial type when reading and spelling, while those with poor verbal scores more often made errors suggesting a phonetic impairment. This is reminiscent of Boder's classification. Kinsbourne and Warrington (1963) selected two small clinic samples of retarded readers one of which had higher performance scores and the other higher verbal scores. They suggested that these represented two distinct aetiological groups, the first having difficulty with sequential ordering, and the second having language abnormalities. This idea was further developed by Nelson and Warrington (1974). They found that in a large group of children retarded in reading and spelling there were more with lower verbal than performance IQs than vice versa. Those with lower verbal IQs showed evidence of generalised reading and spelling problems, while those with lower performance IQs showed relatively normal reading but poor spelling ability. The former group tended to make phonetically inappropriate spelling errors, while the latter group made more phonetically accurate errors. These results support the clinical descriptions of two distinct sub-groups of retarded readers, one having a generalised language problem (being the most common) and the other having a visual perceptual or memory problem.

It seems certain that further research into this possible heterogeneity will be useful. It has been shown there is considerable agreement that there is a group of retarded readers whose problems stem from a language disorder, and another smaller group whose difficulties are of a visuo-perceptual type. Hopefully more precise measures of visual abilities will be combined with studies of the reading and spelling patterns in these children. This should enable better evidence for the 'visual' sub-group to be obtained. For present purposes, however, it is important to point out that the practice in experimental reports of merely giving mean differences between groups only serves to obscure the existence of these putative sub-groups.

Visual abilities

(a) Visual perception.   A good deal of consideration has
been given to the question of whether retarded readers as a
group are deficient in their visual perceptual, as distinct
from visual memory, abilities.   Benton (1962) reviewed the
earlier studies pointing out their inadequacies of design and
contradictory findings.   He concluded that 'deficiency in
visual form perception is not an important correlate of
developmental dyslexia.'   Here emphasis will be given to
more recent studies which do nothing to challenge this
conclusion.

Following Orton's (1937) stress on the prevalence of
orientation errors in the reading and spelling of retarded
readers, a common idea has been that these children may
have difficulty perceiving orientation accurately.   Wechsler
and Hagin (1964) claimed that this was the case.   They gave
a perceptual matching task to an unselected sample of 50
first- and 50 third-grade children in which shapes had to be
matched on the basis of orientation.   Errors on this task
correlated with reading ability in both groups.   No consideration was given to IQ in this study and there is no reason
to suppose that this test was sensitive to anything other than
general intellectual ability.   Furthermore, even if this test
were a genuine correlate of reading ability in the general
population, this would not necessarily be of any relevance to
the problems of retarded readers.   For example, in the
general population intelligence is highly correlated with
reading achievement (Rutter et al., 1970).   It is clear,
however, that this correlation breaks down in the case of
retarded readers.   Some children may be highly intelligent
but have profound difficulties in learning to read.

Doehring (1968) found that retarded readers were inferior
to controls on the Thurstone reversals test.   In this test
pairs of line drawings are shown, some of which are identical while others are mirror image figures.   The child has
to indicate whether each pair is the same or different.   No
details of test administration were given but it seems that a
failure to understand the concept of same and different
properly could be responsible for the retarded readers'
poor performance on this test.   To ask simply if pairs of
drawings are the same when they only differ in orientation
may be ambiguous to children without some non-verbal
demonstration of the difference of relevance.

Stanley, Kaplan and Poole (1975) examined more complex

discriminations of orientation in a visual matching with
spatial transformation test.   Retarded and normal readers
were shown a series of photographs each of which displayed
three complex wooden block forms.   Two of the forms were
in fact identical although their orientation differed.   The
task was to pick the odd one out.   This is a difficult task
probably involving the mental manipulation of orientation and
yet the retarded readers performed this slightly, but non-
significantly, better than the controls.   This is even more
surprising when it is considered that no formal tests of IQ
were given in this study and the selection criteria adopted
may well have resulted in the retarded readers being rather
less intelligent than the controls.

Some studies have suggested that retarded readers are
impaired on measures of visuo-motor co-ordination.   As
mentioned earlier the Isle of Wight study found constructional difficulties were characteristic of this group.   In the
Bender-Gestalt test children are required to copy a series
of geometric forms.   Lachmann (1960) and Satz, Rardin and
Ross (1971) reported that young (8-10 years in one and 7-8
years in the other) retarded readers were impaired on this
test while older retarded readers (11 years plus) were not.
On the other hand Symmes and Rapoport (1972) found no
evidence for visuo-motor difficulty even among young retarded readers as assessed by the Bender test, the Benton
visual retention test (drawing forms from memory) or the
Slosson drawing completion test.   In this study the retarded
readers were carefully selected to exclude any cases with
possible neurological impairment but the assessments were
only made by comparison with published test norms.   Lingren
(1969) also found no differences between normal and retarded
readers (8-14 years old), on the Bender-Gestalt or a test
involving visual matching.   It seems that poor performance
on the Bender test is certainly not a universal correlate of
reading retardation, and in any case the test is not a pure
test of visual perception.   If poor performance on this test
is accepted as a characteristic of young retarded readers,
this may plausibly be related to their immaturity of motor
development described earlier, rather than to their perceptual abilities.   Furthermore, if these difficulties were
causally related to the retarded readers' problems it would
be hard to see why they should experience anything more
than a transitory difficulty which disappeared as their
visual abilities matured.

In the Satz et al. (1971) study the retarded readers per-

formed as well as controls on a test of visual discrimination
which supports the view that any difficulty shown by retarded
readers on the Bender test may not depend on its visual
requirements.  Walters and Doan (1962) found normal performance in retarded readers on a test of visual closure
(identifying incomplete figures) and visual differentiation (a
test devised by Gibson and Gibson (1955) requiring memory
for a form which was to be picked out from amongst a set of
similar forms).  Doehring (1968) reported that retarded
readers were slower on visual search tasks requiring them
to scan arrays of letters, digits and abstract figures and
underline exemplars of a given item.  Slowness on such
timed tasks is hard to interpret in the absence of any more
general evidence of perceptual difficulties.  Learning to
read is not limited by any rigid time constraints.  While
such differences in perceptual speed might account for differences in reading speed, it is hard to see how they could
explain severe and persistent reading problems.

There is actually some evidence that retarded readers
may excel in their visual perceptual abilities.  As mentioned
before, Stanley et al. (1975) found that retarded readers
were slightly better than controls at matching spatial trans-
forms of three-dimensional figures.  Lyle (1968b) compared
the error patterns of retarded and normal readers on the
WISC block design test.  No differences were found.  When
allowance was made for the retarded readers' slightly lower
mean IQ, however, they were found to score significantly
higher on this sub-test than the controls.  Symmes and
Rapoport (1972) also found their group of retarded readers
excelled on tests of visual perceptual ability such as the
WISC object assembly and block design sub-tests.  They
proposed the somewhat exotic idea that there may be a sex-
linked genetic linkage between spatial visualisation and
reading retardation.  This is the opposite of the predominant belief in the field with which we started and goes even
further beyond any available evidence, because many of the
other studies report that retarded readers are slightly worse
on tests of visual ability.  Whatever else is concluded from
these numerous studies, however, it seems certain that for
the majority of retarded readers a simple deficit in the
visual perception of form cannot account for their profound
reading problems.

Further evidence to support this view comes from a longitudinal study.  Robinson and Schwartz (1973) studied 142
5-6-year-old children on their entry to school.  The

Bender-Gestalt test was given to them along with two tests
of visual perception and the Stanford-Binet IQ test.
Forty-one children scored one standard deviation below the
mean on the tests of visual perception or visuo-motor co-
ordination. This 'high risk' group were matched with 23
controls randomly selected from the remaining children who
did not show any perceptual problems; these controls were
slightly, but not significantly, more intelligent. Both
groups were given intensive examinations including neurological assessment, WISC IQ, reading tests and the same
tests of visual and visuo-motor function, at the end of their
third year at school.

The striking finding was that, although the 'high risk'
group was now of lower IQ and had persistent visual problems, it did not differ from the controls in reading attainment. There were 10 children, 9 from the 41 'high risk'
children and 1 from the 23 controls, who had reading quo-
tients below 100. These children were compared with the
rest of the group who were all reading adequately. They
did not differ on any visual or visuo-motor test, but they
were found to be less intelligent. There was thus no evidence that these tests could predict reading attainment.

Finally, one other piece of evidence which also goes
against the idea that visual perceptual difficulties are an
important cause of reading retardation comes from cases of
Turner's syndrome. Although these children characteris-
tically have severe visuo-spatial problems they generally
read adequately (Alexander and Money, 1965).

Recently, Clifton-Everest (1976) has argued that the
failure of studies to demonstrate an impairment in visual
perception amongst retarded readers reflects the fact that
they have ignored the possibility of unique skills being
involved in the visual perception of written language. He
suggests that some retarded readers do not respond faster
in a same/different judgment task to pairs of words than to
random letter strings, while normal readers including
children do show such a facilitation. It was also suggested
that some retarded readers do not search more quickly
within words for pronounceable letter strings than unproun-
ceable letter strings, as normal adults and children do.
Inadequacies in the group studied (only eight retarded
readers of unspecified reading level and IQ) and the reporting of this experiment make it impossible to judge the findings. It does seem advisable, however, for any future
studies of visual perception in retarded readers to look at

tasks more closely related to reading as suggested in this study. If this is done, sophisticated techniques will be required to eliminate the possible influence of verbal factors in the tasks studied. Also, if such experiments are to be interpretable, matching on the basis of reading age would seem mandatory. If this is not done any differences found may just as easily be the effects of poor reading as the cause.

(b) Iconic memory. Sperling (1960) and Averbach and Coriell (1961) obtained evidence for a high capacity, short duration visual memory system later referred to by Neisser (1967) as iconic memory. From these experiments it appears that the visual image is retained in a comparatively raw form for some short time after the stimulus disappears. Some of the information present in this high capacity but short-lived store may then be transferred to a more durable but more limited capacity, short-term memory store. Some studies have examined whether retarded readers have poor iconic memory.

Stanley and Hall (1973) compared the performance of retarded and normal readers in two experiments relevant to this question. In the first, two simple stimuli (e.g. N and O) were presented in rapid succession at the same location in a tachistoscope, the time between them (the ISI) being gradually increased over trials. The children were required to make two judgments, first to say when two elements appeared rather than a single fused image, and second to identify the two elements. The second task is the more difficult and requires a longer ISI than the first. The retarded readers required significantly longer ISIs to do both tasks. Their iconic memories persisted longer than those of the controls. The fact that the retarded readers were also slower on the second task was interpreted as evidence for the slower transfer of information from iconic to short-term memory. The logic behind this suggestion is not clear, however. This second finding would seem to be an inescapable consequence of longer iconic persistence. This longer persistence would naturally lead to more interference between the two stimuli, and so greater difficulty in identifying them.

In a second experiment the same children had to identify a briefly presented (20 msec) letter followed by a dot pattern mask (20 msec duration also). The ISI necessary for correct identification of the letter was measured. The retarded readers again required longer ISIs than the controls. This was also interpreted as evidence for slower transfer of information from iconic to short-term memory.

A later experiment by Stanley (1976) makes this idea seem unlikely, however. In this study single digits were presented tachistoscopically for 20 msec followed by a dot pattern mask at various ISIs from 8 to 40 msec. The subjects responded by pressing a labelled button to indicate the digit that had been presented. The retarded readers here responded slightly faster and significantly more accurately than the controls. This suggests that their difficulty in reporting the letters presented in the Stanley and Hall experiment may have related to the use of a verbal response. A further finding of interest which is consistent with this explanation was that the majority of the retarded readers had an error pattern which suggested the use of a visual code. They made most confusions between digits with curved features while the controls did not show any such consistency.

Essentially identical results concerning visual persistence in retarded readers were reported by Stanley (1975) in a later experiment in which retarded readers required a longer ISI to identify the two separate halves of a cross. In all these studies the use of selection criteria which omitted any direct measure of IQ raises the possibility that at least part of the effect could be due to the likelihood that the retarded readers were somewhat less intelligent than the controls. Such doubts are allayed by a further study in which IQ was measured (O'Neill and Stanley, 1976). In this study the stimuli were simple straight lines. The retarded readers again had longer separation thresholds for pairs of these stimuli. They also required longer exposure durations to detect the presence of a single line presented after a homogenous light mask. Longer visual persistence does therefore appear to be a correlate of reading retardation.

A large question remains as to how to interpret these findings. It is hard to see how a highly durable iconic memory could impede learning to read. Even if the further idea of a slower transfer of information from iconic to short-term memory is accepted, in the absence of any good evidence, it is still hard to envisage how such a difference could retard learning to read. Very similar results have been obtained in the case of mentally retarded children (Thor and Holden, 1969). In this study, series of rapid light flashes were presented to normal and mentally retarded children matched for mental age. Their task was to judge the number of flashes which occurred. The retarded children were particularly bad at this task when the flashes were separated by short ISIs and occurred in the same position on the screen. It appears that they, like retarded readers, have abnormally persistent iconic memories. Furthermore, it is known that the duration of the icon decreases with age (Gummerman and Gray, 1972; Pollack, Ptashne and Carter, 1969). In the light of these findings, and in the absence of any coherent and testable theory of how highly persistent iconic storage might cause reading retardation, the most plausible explanation for all these results is that a long persisting icon is a non-specific correlate of an immature or inefficient central nervous system.

(c) Visual memory. As stressed in the introduction, from the first recognition of children with reading retardation, there was a strong emphasis on visual explanations of their difficulties. In particular Hinshelwood (1917) and Orton (1937) both viewed reading retardation as a failure of visual memory. The evidence derived from the many studies these theories prompted is again mixed and inconclusive but largely negative.

One approach to this problem is in terms of the errors retarded readers make in reading and spelling. Orton's (1937) theory was largely based on his observation of a large number of reversal errors in these children's reading and spelling which he explained in terms of abnormal visual memory processes. He noted two types: 'static' reversals involving single letters, as in writing 'b' for 'd'; and 'kinetic' reversals in which whole sequences of letters were reversed as in reading 'was' for 'saw'. Orton made the claim that these types of errors were more common in the reading and writing of retarded readers than in the errors of normal children of the same reading age. This potentially important observation has not been substantiated in later reports.

Liberman, Shankweiler, Orlando, Harris and Berti (1971) studied the reading errors of a group of children at the bottom of their year for reading attainment in one school. They found that although there was great variability, reversal errors accounted for only a very small proportion of these children's reading errors. The occurrence of static and kinetic reversals in different children did not correlate at all with each other which they argued goes against the assumption implicit in Orton's theory that these errors depend upon the same mechanism.  In their detailed analysis of the errors it seemed that linguistic as well as visual factors were necessary to explain the pattern of results, and they considered that overall the findings argued against Orton's theory.  This conclusion does not follow, however, because of the sample studied.  This was the worst 18 readers out of a population of 59 children.  The children's reading ages were not given and it is not clear that there were any children in the sample particularly retarded in reading.  Although interesting in their own right the findings are not directly relevant to an assessment of Orton's theory of reading retardation.

Other studies have compared the reading and spelling errors of retarded and normal readers and disagreed with Orton's claims about reversal tendencies.  Frank (1936) in a clinical study lacking any quantitative data, reported that the reading and spelling errors of retarded readers were essentially similar to those of younger normal children.  She considered that reversals were probably a function of treating words wholistically rather than being indicative of any pathology.  Tordrup (1966) in a quantitative study of a large sample of retarded readers and younger normals matched for reading age reached the same conclusions.  Reversals were no more common, either absolutely or proportionally, in the errors of retarded readers than of younger normal readers.  One problem with these two studies is that no criteria for classification as a retarded reader are given;  this makes it uncertain how representative the samples were.  Finally, Holmes and Peper (1977) studied the spelling errors of a group of 9–12–year–old retarded readers (reading at least 2 years below their age level) and a group of age matched normal readers.  Although the retarded readers, as expected, made many more spelling errors of all types, the proportions of the different types of errors (which included reversals of the order of letters but not single letter reversals) showed no signs of differences.

It must be concluded that for most retarded readers reversal errors are not a particularly marked characteristic of their reading and spelling.  It remains possible, if unlikely, that such errors are characteristic of some sub–group of retarded readers (cf Boder, 1973) and this deserves further study.  Orton's basic observation upon which his theory of visual memory confusions as a cause of reading retardation was based was almost certainly faulty.  This mistake is perhaps understandable. Retarded readers do make many more errors in reading and spelling than normal children and reversals are particularly striking amongst a host of less easily defined errors. In the light of this early mistake much research on the occurrence of orientation errors in perceptual and memory experiments with these children seems sadly misplaced.

Other evidence comes from experimental studies of visual memory. Some studies have employed tests of drawing from memory. The same problem applies to these as to the Bender-Gestalt test, namely that poor performance may be due to motor rather than visual problems. Findings with these tests as with the Bender have been inconsistent. Lyle (1968a) found that retarded readers were worse than controls at drawing geometric designs from memory when a scoring system which stressed reversals was used, but not on an alternative system which gave equal weight to other distortions. On the other hand Symmes and Rapoport (1972) found their group of retarded readers performed adequately on a test requiring drawing from memory.

Tests of visual recognition are preferable since here any deficits cannot be due to motor difficulties. As mentioned before Walters and Doan (1962) found essentially normal performance by retarded readers on a test of visual differentiation (Gibson and Gibson, 1955). Whipple and Kodman (1969) claimed that retarded readers were worse on this task than controls, but they failed to take account of IQ differences between these groups.

Lyle and Goyen in a series of experiments have compared memory for tachistoscopically presented stimuli in normal and retarded readers. In the first (Lyle and Goyen, 1968) letters, line forms and rectangular shapes representing word outlines were presented. Recognition was tested by having the subject point to the form presented from amongst a five-choice array printed on a card. The retarded readers were worse on all types of material and this effect was most marked amongst the younger children. Subsequent experiments investigated this effect. Goyen and Lyle (1971a) confirmed that the effect only held for young (less than 8.5 years old) retarded readers, and that incentives did not improve their performance which was interpreted as evidence against a motivational explanation of the effect. Goyen and Lyle (1973) then investigated whether the effect was due to a difficulty remembering the stimulus for long enough to make the response. This possibility was

rejected because the retarded readers had an equivalent
difficulty judging whether two rapidly presented geometric
forms were the same or different.   In a final experiment,
Lyle and Goyen (1975) investigated the effects of the speed of
exposure and the difficulty of the discrimination required at
recognition testing in the original paradigm.   It was found
that the retarded readers could perform the task if the
exposure time was lengthened but that the difficulty of the
discrimination had no differential effect on the performance
of the two groups.   We are left then with a very restricted
deficit;  young but not older retarded readers have a specific difficulty in recognising very rapidly presented visual
stimuli.   Following the same line of reasoning as before,
it seems hard to envisage how this could be a cause of reading retardation.   Difficulties which are restricted to young
retarded readers do not seem promising explanations of
enduring reading problems and, more importantly, reading
does not require the recognition of rapidly presented stimuli
as in these experiments.   The most parsimonious explanation of these findings, as in the case of iconic memory differences, appears to be in terms of some general immaturity
of brain function which hampers the processing of very rapid
stimuli.

This interpretation is supported by several studies which
indicate adequate performance by retarded readers on visual
memory tasks which are plainly more similar to reading than
these.   Goyen and Lyle (1971b) in a study with the same
groups of retarded and normal readers found no differences
on a visual paired associate learning task.   This same
finding of normal visual paired associate learning, using
different stimuli, has also been obtained in experiments by
Vellutino and his colleagues (Vellutino, Steger and Pruzek,
1973;  Vellutino, Harding, Phillips and Steger, 1975).

A pattern of normal visual memory abilities amongst
retarded readers emerges from a series of other experiments by Vellutino and his group.   Vellutino, Steger and
Kandel (1972) had normal and retarded readers copy from
memory designs, digit strings, letter strings and words.
The two groups performed equally with the non-verbal
stimuli, but ceiling effects were in evidence here.   Performance on the verbal materials was more variable but the
retarded readers were only significantly worse at copying
the longer words, and they copied all words much better
than they could read them.   The results implied that a
verbal rather than a visual problem characterised the
retarded readers.

In a more impressive experiment Vellutino, Pruzek, Steger and Meshoulam (1973) showed Hebrew words to normal and retarded readers who were not learning to read Hebrew and to a group of normal readers who were learning Hebrew. The children had to draw from memory the letters they remembered after a brief presentation on a screen in front of them. There were no differences in visual recall between the normal and retarded readers, but the children learning Hebrew did perform better than either of these two groups, especially on the longer words. This pattern was reminiscent of the retarded readers' difficulty with longer words in the previous experiment. A second experiment replicated the findings of this study with a group of younger retarded readers (8.5 years old) to take account of the evidence reviewed earlier that visual problems may be more common amongst young retarded readers. Once again there were no differences in visual recall between normal and retarded readers (Vellutino, Steger, Kaman and DeSetto, 1975).

In a further experiment (Vellutino, Steger, DeSetto and Phillips, 1975) the possibility of long-term visual memory difficulties as a cause of reading retardation was examined in a similar design. In this case memory for Hebrew letters was assessed by means of recognition either immediately after presentation or after twenty-four hour, and six month delays. The retarded and normal readers again showed no differences in performance in any of the conditions.

In the light of these findings the idea of a visual memory deficit as a cause of reading retardation seems highly implausible. In tasks which are demonstrably similar to reading in their visual requirements normal and retarded readers consistently perform at similar levels.

In these studies by Vellutino and his group, memory for order was involved but no differences were found. Two studies explicitly dealing with memory for the order of visual stimuli have claimed there are differences between normal and retarded readers. Stanley, Kaplan and Poole (1975) gave normal and retarded readers a test of visual sequential memory from the Illinois Test of Psycholinguistic Abilities. The retarded readers performed this poorly, but as already mentioned it is quite likely that these groups differed in IQ as well as reading ability. Furthermore, this test may involve verbal memory abilities. Kirk and Kirk (1971) who devised the ITPA note that the visual sequential memory test may sometimes be performed by using a verbal memory strategy. They even suggest that difficulties in performing the test may be eleviated by training such strategies. Both these observations suggest that the retarded readers' difficulties on this test may relate to their verbal rather than visual problems. As we will see later Blank and Bridger (1966) have shown that retarded readers may be particularly bad at generating verbal descriptions of abstract configurations of this sort.

The second study (Noelker and Schumsky, 1973) contains similar flaws. The difference in IQ between the normal and retarded readers approached significance in this study and the task that showed the greatest difference between the groups, memory for a series of white and black circles, almost certainly involved verbal mediation. Another complication in this study is the use of a delay in which the subjects had to count aloud. In view of the evidence reviewed later of language and speech problems in retarded readers, it seems likely that this task would be more difficult for them and so might account for some of the differences in performance that were found.

In conclusion, it seems there is no evidence that a deficit in visual memory is a cause of the majority of retarded readers' problems. This brings us back to the problem of different types of reading retardation, however. In many of these studies the retarded readers perform slightly, but not significantly, worse than the controls. It remains a strong possibility therefore that a sub-group of retarded readers do suffer from visual memory difficulties. Further work will be necessary to identify this sub-group with any certainty.


Cross-modal abilities

A second approach to the causes of reading retardation has looked at cross-modal abilities. Learning to read involves making an association between visual and auditory stimuli. The child has to learn that visually presented written words and letters signify particular sounds in spoken language. If a child was unable to make such associations he would be unable to learn to read. The many studies dealing with this question have been critically reviewed by Bryant (1975). Consequently, only a brief account of the major findings will be given here.

These studies start with the work of Birch and Belmont (1964).  They thought that difficulties in linking auditory and visual information might be a cause of poor reading, at least in some cases.  To test this idea they compared a large group of retarded readers with a group of controls on an auditory-visual matching task.  On each trial the experimenter tapped out a pattern on the desk, the interval between each pair of taps being either long or short.  After this the child was shown three visual patterns each composed of dots arranged in a straight line, the only difference being in the length of the gaps between the dots.  The child had to pick the visual pattern which matched the pattern of taps he had just heard, i.e., match an auditory-temporal pattern with a visual-spatial one.  The results were quite straightforward. The retarded readers were worse on this task than the controls, and many subsequent studies have confirmed the reliability of this finding (e.g. Beery, 1967;  Bryden, 1972; Vande Voort, Senf and Benton, 1972).

There are obvious problems of interpretation here.  As no within-modal matching conditions were included, the difficulty may be one of visual or auditory perception rather than of cross-modal integration.  There might also be a conceptual problem in matching temporal and spatial patterns.  Several experiments (e.g. Muehl and Kremenak, 1966;  Blank and Bridger, 1966;  Vande Voort et al., 1972) tried to sort out these two problems.

The most complete of these is that of Bryden (1972). Here visual-temporal sequences - a light flashing on and off at various intervals - were included to assess the difficulty of the temporal-spatial transformation, and within as well as cross-modal conditions were also included.  The nine possible combinations of auditory sequential patterns, visual sequential patterns, and visual spatial patterns were presented to groups of normal and retarded readers who judged whether each pair of patterns were the same or different.

The retarded readers were worse on all nine matching tasks.  There was no sign of them being particularly bad on cross-modal tasks, and in fact the largest difference in performance between the groups appeared in the auditory within-modal condition.

It seems from this that the deficiency revealed in the Birch and Belmont study has nothing to do with the cross-modal integration of information as such.  Retarded readers are generally poor on matching tasks of this type.

We therefore need an explanation of their difficulty on

such tasks. A likely but unproven explanation is that the
have difficulty describing these patterns. Blank and
Bridger (1966) found that retarded readers were bad at
matching temporal and spatial visual sequences. When they
asked the children how they matched these sequences, they
all (normal and retarded readers) said they did so on the
basis of verbal descriptions of the patterns, e.g. two space
two, space one. When simply asked to describe visual
temporal sequences the retarded readers were significantly
less accurate than the normal readers. Such inaccuracy
seems a likely explanation for their difficulties on all these
matching tasks.

One objection to this whole line of research is that the
type of cross-modal integration being dealt with is quite different to that involved in learning to read. These experiments are concerned with 'natural' (Bryant, 1975) cross-
modal associations – the child is required to match auditory
and visual patterns on the basis of an implicit and already
known equivalence between temporal and spatial extent (this
relationship was never trained or made explicit in any other
way to the children in any of these experiments). Reading
is quite different to this. Here we are dealing with a process of learning arbitrary associations between the particular visual configurations of letters and words and their
spoken equivalents. In psychological parlance we are
dealing with visual-verbal paired associate learning. It
could be that retarded readers are particularly bad at learning such cross-modal associations. If they were, this
would clearly make learning to read difficult.

This more precise version of the corss-modal deficit
hypothesis is also almost certainly wrong. If we look at
visual-verbal paired associate learning (PAL), where the
child has to learn nonsense syllable names for arbitrary
shapes, retarded readers are bad at this (Gascon and Goodglass, 1970; Vellutino, Bentley and Phillips, 1978; Vellutino, Steger, Harding and Phillips, 1975). It appears that
this deficit is one of verbal learning. Retarded readers are
also bad on tactual-verbal and auditory-verbal PAL tasks
(Rudel, Denckla and Spalten, 1976). In contrast they consistently perform normally on non-verbal PAL tasks, as in
learning to associate pairs of visual nonsense shapes (Goyen
and Lyle, 1971b; Vellutino, Steger and Pruzek, 1973;
Vellutino, Harding, Phillips and Steger, 1975), learning to
associate visual nonsense shapes with non-verbal sounds
(Vellutino, Steger, Harding and Phillips, 1975) or visual

nonsense shapes with tactile (textural) stimuli (Steger, Vellutino and Meshoulam, 1972). The absence of any generalised intra- or cross-modal associative learning deficit is shown by the finding that in a non-verbal PAL task, normal and retarded readers showed near identical performance in visual-visual, visual-auditory and auditory-auditory learning (Vellutino, Steger and Pruzek, 1973). There is no generalised within or cross-modal associative learning deficit. There is, however, a difficulty with PAL tasks with a verbal component, and as we saw above a likely explanation for their poor performance in the matching tasks was their poor verbal abilities.

In conclusion it seems that retarded readers do not have any particular difficulty in the integration of information from different sensory modalities. Once again it remains possible that a few do have difficulties of this type, but there is really no evidence to even suggest that this is so. The research in this area is not totally negative, however, since both the matching and PAL studies point to some form of language difficulty being an important correlate of reading retardation. It is to a fuller consideration of this idea that we now turn.


Language and auditory perceptual abilities

Although language abilities (such as verbal memory and vocabulary knowledge) are clearly distinguishable in principle from auditory perceptual abilities (such as the ability to segment speech into syllables or to appreciate the similarities between rhyming words), in the research on reading retardation this distinction is often not clearly drawn. Virtually all the work on auditory abilities is concerned with speech perception and so is relevant to an assessment of both auditory and language abilities. Research in these two closely related areas will, therefore, be dealt with together here.

The distinction between auditory and language skills, though generally blurred in this literature, is probably worth emphasising. There may be auditory abilities which are necessary for effectively learning to read, which are not necessary for effectively using oral language. For example, there are suggestions that retarded readers may have particular difficulty in explicitly analysing spoken words into their constituent phonemes (Savin, 1972). This might plausibly cause their reading problems by hampering their understanding of the correspondence between phonemes and the letters in words which they must read. Such fine grained speech analysis is, however, probably quite superfluous to learning to use and understand speech. Conversely, the demonstrated language problems of retarded readers might be at least partially dependent on deficiencies in their auditory abilities. Poor aduitory perception could presumably impair a child's oral language development.

Although the importance of language skills in learning to read should be obvious, consideration of their role has not been predominant in work on reading retardation. Learning to read is a mammoth feat of verbal memory. In more general terms it follows on from and utilises the child's already well developed oral language abilities. An appreciation of phonics enables a child to utilise this knowledge by supplying a strategy for translating written language into its spoken form. This allows new words to be deciphered; self-instruction may take place. It also reveals the redundancies present in written language. Similar sounding words often look alike because their spelling follows the same rules which specify how sounds are represented by letters. Without an appreciation of such redundancy learning to read becomes very difficult, because each new word must be learnt as a unique entity, greatly increasing the load on memory. It is of interest that teachers' descriptions of retarded readers often convey that an inability to understand the relatedness of similar words is one of their characteristics. In addition, comparative studies of reading in different countries have suggested that the more regular the correspondence between letters and sounds in a given language the less likely children are to experience difficulties in learning to read (Downing, 1973).

Another line of evidence which demonstrates the importance of linguistic and auditory perceptual abilities in learning to read is the study of deaf children. They experience profound difficulties in learning to read although the details of why this is so remain open to speculation (Conrad, 1977). What is even more remarkable in this group, however, is that those deaf children who appear to utilise a speech based code for memorising words learn to read significantly better than others who do not do so (Conrad, 1979). So, in a group who more than anyone might be expected to find ways of depending entirely on vision in reading an awareness of speech sounds does in fact seem to be very important for

learning to read.   Less dramatically within the general
school population partial hearing loss is also associated
with retarded reading development (Henry, 1947;  Hine,
1970).

Auditory and language abilities are likely then to be
important determinants of how easily children learn to read.
We turn now to consider research into their role in the
causation of reading retardation.

(a)  Speech perception:  (i) Speech sound discrimination.
Several types of study show that retarded readers have
difficulty in accurately perceiving speech.   First are
studies of speech sound discrimination.   Invariably these
have employed the Wepman (1958) Test of Auditory Discrimination.   The test comes in two parallel forms and each consists of forty pairs of single syllable words.   Thirty pairs
differ by one phoneme while ten are identical and the child
is required to make a same/different judgment as each pair
is read to him by the examiner.   The lack of balance
between same and different pairs is unfortunate since it may
induce a response bias in subjects, due to the tendency to
equate same and different responses in such situations.
Vellutino, DeSetto and Steger (1972) have shown that response bias increases the number of same responses given to
the Wepman test, and thus the test is liable to underestimate
the subject's discriminative ability.

The almost universal finding with this test is that poor
reading ability is associated with poor auditory discrimination.   In normal first grade subjects, Wepman test performance correlated 0.37 with reading test scores which was
higher than the correlation of 0.29 between reading and IQ
(Machowsky and Meyers, 1975).   In studies contrasting
retarded and normal readers the same pattern is evident;
poor readers generally perform poorly (e.g. Deutsch, 1964;
Lingren, 1969;  Clark, 1970;  but see Naidoo, 1972, for an
exception).   De Hirsh, Jansky and Langford (1966) in a
longitudinal study found that performance on this test in
kindergarten was one of the best predictors of subsequent
reading difficulties, when children were tested two years
later.

The question remains to interpret the retarded readers'
poor performance on the Wepman test.   The paired comparison procedure utilised in this test clearly involves complex processes;  each pair of items must be attended to,
retained, compared and a vocal same/different response
made.   Thus, we cannot conclude that poor test performance
necessarily reflects poor speech perception.

The only systematic attempt to examine the factors involved in performing the Wepman test is that of Blank (1968). In the first part of this study it was confirmed that a sample of Israeli children (average age 7 years) showed the typical relation between reading and Wepman test performance. This, and all subsequent parts of the study, are marred by two methodological errors; most important, no control of IQ was made, and second, reading ability was merely assessed on the basis of teacher ratings. Consequently, any relationship between reading ability and test performance is confounded with the probable IQ differences between the groups. In addition teachers' ratings of reading are likely to be less than totally accurate.

In the second part of the study, two further groups selected on the same basis from the normal school population were asked to repeat the word pairs without making same/different judgments. Here two different measures were computed, the number of words correctly repeated, and by extrapolation from the child's responses the number of same/different responses expected to be correct, i.e., if the pair presented was different the child was credited with one pair correct if he said two different words, even though the words may have differed from the stimulus pair. The poor readers were worse on both of these measures suggesting a genuine perceptual difficulty. Further analysis revealed that the poor reader group made disproportionately more wrong pair answers than did the normals, and that this was due to a perseveration tendency merely to repeat the first word in a pair. Such responses are difficult to evaluate. Blank suggests they may indicate poor attention. Equally plausibly, if the child has perceptual difficulty, an easy way to satisfy the task requirement is to repeat the first word. This is especially true if this difficulty centres on the perception of sounds at the ends of sequences. (Note in this regard the tendency of these children to make most errors on pairs which differ on the end sound.)

In the third experiment, the test words were presented one at a time with similar sounding words in non-adjacent positions, and the child was required to repeat each word after it had been presented. In this condition the poor readers performed slightly, but not significantly, worse than the normals. In such undemanding conditions the perception of single words is apparently not impaired in this group of poor readers who may, however, not be comparable to other samples of retarded readers in the severity of their reading problem.  No data on reading achievement are given which can be used to assess this.

As previously pointed out, the failure to control for IQ, and the crude assessment of reading ability in this study, makes it impossible to draw any conclusions about the specific correlates of reading ability from the data. Nevertheless these results suggest that other factors apart from the perception of the individual words presented influence performance on the Wepman test.  Just how these factors operate is not clarified, however.  In the first experiment it is suggested that the same/different judgment presents difficulties.  Several children dropped out of the study due to an inability to understand the task, and unfortunately, no data on the reading ages of these children is presented. · Difficulties of understanding the test have not been reported previously and Wepman considers the test suitable for younger children than those studied here (7 year olds).  Such failures seem surprising, and one wonders whether the testing was carried out inadequately, or whether the children were of particularly low IQ.

It seems little can be said about the critical features of the Wepman test which cause problems for normal children, or those that allow it to differentiate normal from retarded readers.  The striking fact is the similarity of the pattern of errors for normal and retarded readers (Naidoo's findings, and my own pilot study with a similar test).  This demonstrates that the stimuli which cause consistent errors to be made by retarded readers and normals are difficult for all children to process whether at a perceptual or at a mnemonic level.

(ii) Rhyming.  Another speech perception task which differentiates normal and retarded readers is their ability to perceive rhymes or in more general terms to appreciate the similarities between words which have certain sounds in common.  Doehring (1968) found that retarded readers were much less successful when asked to produce words which rhymed with a spoken word than normals.  Similarly, Supramaniam and Audley (1976) found that retarded readers were slower than controls to decide if letter or picture pairs had the same name or had names that rhymed.  This difference was much more marked in the rhyming condition, however.  In both these cases, it is not clear whether a perceptual ability is being tapped or a facet of the retarded reader's word finding difficulty (see below for some evidence on this).  Savin (1972) on the basis of informal observations, noted that retarded readers were peculiarly insensitive to rhymes that they heard.

This difficulty with rhymes does appear to be a perceptual problem which cannot be explained as a mere consequence of limited reading ability or experience. Bradley and Bryant (1978) showed that retarded readers were worse at detecting a non-rhyming word which they heard spoken in a group of three other rhyming words than younger normal children of the same reading age and IQ. The same pattern was true for words which shared the same initial or middle phoneme, in fact the difference was most marked in the former condition. Teachers' impressions that these children are unable to understand the relatedness of similar sounding words are clearly well founded, and these results suggest that such a difficulty may be a cause of these children's reading problems.

Broadly speaking there would appear to be two possible causes of the retarded readers' difficulty on tests of rhyming. One is that they have difficulty in categorising sounds on the basis of their acoustic similarity. Another explanation might be in terms of speech segmentation. The ability to hear rhymes may depend upon being able to segment speech into its constituent phonemes. In order to detect a rhyme one must realise that the sounds at the end of the rhyming words are the same. Some studies have looked directly at this ability and its relationship to reading. Although it seems likely that retarded readers are also bad on such tasks, according to the evidence presented below it seems unlikely that their difficulties on these two tasks depend on the same mechanism.

(iii) Speech segmentation. Research in this area takes its rationale from consideration of those functions which the child must perform in order to take full advantage of an alphabetic script, i.e., to map the printed word 'bag' on to its spoken counterpart he must realise that the spoken syllable also has three segments. It must be emphasised that in the course of normal speech there is no such requirement and words are probably perceived in units which are at least a syllable in length, and not as conglomerations of phonemes. Rather, it appears that phonemes are in a sense synthetic units which are inferred following recognition of the larger pattern of the syllable. This argument has been advanced by Warren (1976). The evidence which supports it cannot be fully discussed here, but depends on two major types of finding. First, in identification time experiments it has been found that it takes longer to identify a phoneme than the entire syllable containing the phoneme (Savin and Bever, 1970; Warren, 1971).   Furthermore, when the context of sentences is varied to accelerate or retard the identification of a word, the times required for the identification of constituent phonemes are changed correspondingly (Warren, 1971).   In another set of experiments it has been shown that when individual phonemes are deleted from the speech signal, this cannot be detected and observers report hearing the deleted phonemes clearly.   Apparently their presence is inferred from the context (Warren, 1970; Warren and Obusek, 1971;  Warren and Sherman, 1974).

The relation between the ability to segment speech into phonemes and reading ability has been investigated by I. Liberman and her colleagues (Liberman, Shankweiler, Fischer and Carter, 1974).   In a normative study of 4-, 5- and 6-year-old boys, the task was to segment speech into either syllables or phonemes which the children indicated by tapping out the number of such segments (1-3) present in each of a series of words which were read to them. Syllable segmentation was much easier than phoneme seg- mentation at all ages.   At age 4 years none could segment phonemically, while at age 6 years, 70 per cent could do so. The corresponding figures for syllable segmentation were 50 per cent and 90 per cent.   A follow-up study showed that performance on the phoneme segmentation task correlated with subsequent reading achievement (Liberman, Shankweiler, Liberman, Fowler and Fischer, 1977).   This finding is hard to interpret, however, since no account of IQ was taken in this study.   Liberman et al. consider the fact that poor and early readers typically make more errors on consonants at the ends of words (Liberman, 1973), when reading is also consistent with a deficiency in speech segmentation ability.   According to this view success in reading initial letters in words is due to the fact that the sound of the initial letter is available without further segmentation of the syllable.   It would be useful to extend this work on phonemic segmentation to the study of retarded readers. It seems likely, according to informal observations (Savin, 1972), that these children would have particular difficulty on this task.

As pointed out before, it is possible that the rhyming and phoneme segmentation tasks both tap the same ability.   An inability to segment speech may disrupt the perception of rhymes.   If this were the sole difficulty, however, one would expect, on the basis of the Liberman argument, that poor readers should be better at identifying words with common beginnings (i.e., in identifying that 'sun', 'sock' and 'see' are similar because the share the same first sound while 'rag' does not) than they are at detecting rhymes (i.e., in identifying that 'weed', 'need' and 'deed' are similar, while 'peel' is not) because the initial sound in a spoken word is supposed to be available to the child without segmenting the syllable. Bradley and Bryant, in their study, found that the converse is true, however. The hardest condition in their experiment for the retarded readers was to pick out the odd word from a group of three others which all shared the same initial phoneme (e.g. sun, sock, see, rag). This task gave a larger difference between the normal and retarded readers than the rhyming task (e.g. weed, need, deed, peel). This is the opposite pattern of results to that expected if this task depends upon segmenting speech into phonemes, given that the Liberman argument about the irrelevance of speech segmentation to detecting the initial phonemes in words is correct.

In connection with this, it is also interesting to consider that most errors on the Wepman test are reported to occur with word pairs which differ only in their endings (Blank, 1968). The fact that the reading errors and speech discrimination errors of poor readers both predominate at the ends of words prompts us to consider whether a common mechanism is involved. It seems that we cannot invoke the previously advanced speech segmentation deficit to explain the discrimination errors, since according to arguments presented previously, discrimination between word pairs ought to be possible without resorting to phonemic analysis. If this is true, either the speech segmentation explanation of the reading error pattern is wrong or the similarity of the reading and speech discrimination error patterns does not derive from a common mechanism.

(b) Auditory perception. One might ask whether the speech perception difficulties of retarded readers, and also perhaps their generalised language difficulties, depend on some generalised auditory impairment in the same way that it has been suggested that the abnormalities of speech development in aphasic children may depend upon an auditory impairment (e.g. Tallal and Piercy, 1973a; 1973b; 1974; 1975). There are not sufficient data to assess this at present, but it appears to be a promising area for study.

One approach to this is in studies of the perception of

rhythmic sequences.  The first method which appears to
have been applied in this field is that of imitation.  Here
the tester taps out a pattern and the child attempts to
imitate it.  Stambak (1951) was apparently the first to
report that reading disturbed children 7-14 years old were
poor on this task, and that they showed less improvement on
it with age than normals.  Unfortunately, no control of IQ
appears to have been included in this study.

De Hirsch, Jansky and Langford (1966) included a tapped
rhythm imitation test as one of a battery of screening
devices administered to kindergarten children as possible
predictors of reading failure two years later.  Close
inspection shows that the significant relation reported
between these two measures was only marked in the case of
girls.  Because the test scores were not normally distributed they were analysed by non-parametric statistical tests.
These did not permit the use of partial correlational techniques, and it was therefore impossible in this study to
assess the relevance of IQ to such scores.

Blank, Weider and Bridger (1968) studied rhythm imitation in two groups of 6-7-year-old retarded and normal
readers who were matched for IQ.  The patterns, containing from 2 to 10 items, were presented vocally by a music
teacher who then scored the child's imitative responses,
only 'exact' imitations being allowed as correct.  Little
difference was found; ten test series were presented, the
mean number of errors for retarded readers was three
(range 0-6) and for controls the mean error score was two
(range 0-5).  However, this was a small sample (two groups
of 12) and the young ages studied meant they had little reading experience on which to base judgments of reading
retardation.

It must be concluded that there is no unambiguous evidence
that poor reading ability is associated with poor ability to
imitate rhythms.  In addition, the imitation test does not
seem a particularly good way of investigating rhythm perception since it confounds perception and production factors.

Preferable in this respect are studies using a same/
different judgment procedure.  The only studies using such
a procedure have not been explicitly concerned with rhythm
perception at all, but have addressed the problem of cross-
modal integration in retarded readers.

Studies comparing retarded and normal readers have
found that the former are deficient in rhythm matching tasks.
Zurif and Carson (1970) and Vande Voort, Senf and Benton

(1972) compared normal and retarded readers on auditory
and visual rhythm matching tests. In both these studies,
the retarded readers were worse on both tests than the
normals. Bryden (1972) compared normal and retarded
readers on several rhythm matching tasks. The retarded
readers were significantly worse on the matching of auditory rhythmic patterns, and worse, though not significantly,
on matching visual rhythms.

It seems safe to conclude that retarded readers are
impaired in judging the equivalence of auditory and probably
also of visual rhythmic patterns. The question of the exact
nature of this difficulty is still obscure. As mentioned
before, Blank (Blank and Bridger, 1966; Blank, Weider and
Bridger, 1968) has suggested this deficit may reflect a
deficiency in the verbal coding of temporal sequences, and
this hypothesis is certainly appealing. Because of the
likelihood of verbal mediation being involved in performing
these tasks, they can tell us nothing directly about auditory
perceptual abilities, although it is interesting to note that
the retarded readers tend to have more difficulty in matching
the auditory temporal sequences than visual temporal
sequences to each other. Since here presumably the
language coding requirements are the same, some sort of
auditory perceptual deficit is implicated.

There seems very little evidence indeed from studies
which do not confound auditory and language abilities. As
mentioned earlier, Vellutino, Steger and Pruzek (1973)
found that retarded readers performed normally on a non-
verbal auditory paired associate learning task. The only
positive evidence in the area comes from a very brief report
of an experiment by Tallal (1976). She reports that some
retarded readers have difficulties perceiving rapid auditory
sequences of the type which aphasic children also find difficult to perceive. It seems likely that further research on
this question would be fruitful.

(c) Language abilities. There is a great deal of evidence
showing an association between oral language difficulties
and reading retardation. Delays and abnormalities of
speech development are common among retarded readers.
In the Isle of Wight study (Rutter et al., 1970) parental
reports indicated that retarded readers were slower than
controls in uttering their first words and in using simple
phrases. Poorly developed speech was also in evidence in
a structured interview given to each child at the age of 9-10
years. Here more retarded readers were found to have

articulation difficulties than controls. They also
showed poorer syntax and were less adept in their use of
descriptive language. Other surveys support these observations. Clark (1970) and Morris (1966) found that speech
defects were more common among backward readers. Lyle
(1970) also found that speech delay and speech defects were
associated with reading retardation.

The likelihood of these language abnormalities being
causally responsible for reading problems is bolstered by
the findings of longitudinal studies. Ingram (1970) in a
study of children presenting with speech delay before starting school found that one third experienced difficulties with
reading or spelling after two years of school, a rate much
higher than in a group of matched controls. De Hirsch,
Jansky and Langford (1966) found several measures of oral
language development at kindergarten level to be predictive
of later reading problems two and a half years later.

Another line of evidence which is relevant here is the
finding mentioned earlier (p. 20), that an excess of retarded
readers perform better on the performance than on the
verbal sub-scales of the WISC. Population surveys again
give the most reliable evidence here, because any differences cannot be due to sampling biases. In the Isle of Wight
study more retarded readers had significantly lower verbal
than performance IQs, as assessed by a short version of
the WISC, than did the controls. Similar results were
reported in surveys of poor readers by Belmont and Birch
(1966) and Clark (1970). Many other studies of more highly
selected groups of retarded readers also find this pattern
(e.g. Doehring, 1968; Nelson and Warrington, 1974).
These findings, then, indicate some impairment of general
language skills amongst retarded readers, although, as
pointed out earlier in the discussion of the possible sub-
groups of retarded readers, this pattern is certainly not
universal.

(d) Verbal memory. Apart from this evidence for generally poor language skills there are an extensive number of
reports showing deficiencies in verbal memory amongst
retarded readers. As stated earlier, reading is certainly
an impressive feat of verbal memory. Difficulties in this
area must, therefore, be likely causes of reading retardation.

(i) Digit span. A measure of digit span is one of the
verbal sub-tests of the WISC. In this the examiner says a
series of digits ranging from two at a time upwards until the

child fails to repeat two successive lists in the correct
serial order. A similar procedure is followed for backward
span, where the digits must be repeated in the reverse order.
Although there is evidence for distinct skills being involved
in these two tasks (Rudel and Denckla, 1974) the digit span
score is based on a joint score from both.

There are many reports that retarded readers are particularly bad on this test. For example, McLeod (1965) found
that a group of retarded readers scored significantly lower
on this sub-test than a group of normal readers after allowing for IQ differences between the groups. Many other
studies (reviewed by Huelsman, 1970) have reported low
digit span scores in groups of retarded readers, but this is
certainly not an invariable finding. For example, although
Lyle and Goyen (1969) reported that their group of retarded
readers had low digit span scores in comparison with controls this difference was not significant. Furthermore, as
Huelsman stresses, group differences between normal and
retarded readers on WISC sub-tests conceal great individual
variability within these groups. Nevertheless, there is
good evidence that on average retarded readers do more
poorly on this test.

None of these reports appears to have considered possible
differences between the backward and forward spans.
Corkin (1974) in an experimental study found that retarded
readers had lower forward spans for auditory digit lists than
a group of controls. It seems, therefore, that the low
spans often found in reports of WISC profiles do not depend
solely on the requirements of the backward span task.
Poor recall of auditory digit strings appears to be part of a
generalised verbal memory deficit amongst retarded readers
as will be further documented below.

Differences on the digit span have sometimes been taken
as evidence for a specific difficulty in handling sequential
information (e.g. Corkin, 1974). This does not follow,
however. In order to demonstrate a particular difficulty
with memory for order in this situation it would be necessary
to compare ordered and free recall. No study appears to
have done this and the present studies do not permit any
specific conclusions to be drawn about memory for order in
retarded readers.

(ii) Verbal sequential memory. This idea of a possible
deficit in order memory amongst retarded readers is a persistent one. Some experiments on visual sequential memory
have already been reviewed. The cross-modal matching

studies are also relevant here since they involve the matching of sequences. The rationale of studies of sequential
perception and memory has been that an inability to remember sequences, such as the sequences of phonemes and
letters that compose spoken and written words, would
hinder learning to read. Memory for the order of letters
in words is obviously a requirement for successful reading
and perhaps more so for spelling. Although this approach
is a reasonable one there seems a danger of the concept of
sequencing ability becoming reified. It was argued that
the cross-modal matching studies were best explained in
terms of a difficulty with verbal memory coding. Similarly,
with the studies of visual sequential memory it was not clear
that verbal difficulties had been ruled out as an explanation
of the findings. In the studies reviewed below, dealing
with memory for visually presented verbal sequences a
verbal memory problem is also demonstrated. It will also
be argued that as in the case of the studies referred to
above, a specific deficit in memory for order has not yet
been demonstrated in these studies.

In the earliest study of this type, Bakker (1967) compared
two groups of retarded readers, one group being two years
behind age norms in reading, the other four years behind.
Each subject was shown several groups of four items pro-
jected in temporal succession. Four types of stimuli were
used: nonsense figures, meaningful figures, letters and
digits. After each series the subject was shown a card on
which all four stimuli were present, and asked to indicate
the order of their presentation. The more severely retarded readers were only worse on the letters and meaningful
figure sequences. Bakker suggests a deficiency in verbal
memory amongst the worse readers as an explanation of the
results. This seems plausible, although the absence of a
difference on the digit sequences seems a problem for this
explanation. Since no normal control group was included
in this study no conclusions about reading retardation can
be drawn.

In a similar study Bakker (1972) presented temporal
sequences of letter triplets visually, auditorily or haptically. Following each series just two of the letters were
presented again and the child had to indicate orally the
order in which they had been presented. Subjects here
were a group of normal and a group of retarded readers.
The retarded readers were worse on all three tasks, but
the groups also differed in IQ. To exclude this possible

explanation of the results two groups of fourteen retarded and normal readers were individually matched for IQ. When this was done the same differences were still evident.

Leslie (1975) made a further study of retarded and normal readers in a variant of the Bakker serial memory task. In this case, on each of six trials, six pictures of common objects were presented in a different order. After each presentation a set of the same pictures had to be arranged to indicate the order in which they had been presented. Performance on the first trial did not differ between the groups. The performance of both decreased over trials but this was much more marked in the case of the retarded readers. This decline appeared to be due to proactive interference, because when on the seventh trial a novel set of six pictures was shown, both groups' performance increased so that they again performed at a similar level. The reasons for this pattern of results is not clear but Leslie suggests that a deficiency in verbal memory coding in the retarded readers was responsible. No evidence in support of this interpretation is provided, however.

It seems that retarded readers are worse in their short term memory for verbal sequences than normal readers, but this difference probably only appears after repeated presentations of the same material. These studies do not, however, provide evidence for a specific deficit in memory for order as is claimed. Failures of item memory would also lead to this pattern of results. By definition you cannot remember the position of items if the items themselves are forgotten. In order to draw conclusions about memory for order per se from experiments of this kind it would be necessary to show that the memory load for the groups compared was equal. For example, one could give measures of memory span for the items concerned to the two groups, and use such measures to equate the difficulty level of the task for them. Such a procedure has never been used and, because of this, conclusions about specific difficulties in order memory are unwarranted.

One other study must also be mentioned which has explicitly considered order memory in retarded readers. Corkin (1974) compared the ability of normal and retarded readers to imitate the order in which the experimenter tapped a series of wooden blocks, either immediately or after a 6-second delay during which the blocks were covered. The retarded readers were worse at this, but only after a delay. Again little can be said with any certainty about the causes of this difference.  It is, however, compatible with the idea advanced earlier that retarded readers have difficulty remembering events in terms of verbal descriptions.  It seems quite plausible to suggest that when a response could be made immediately a non-verbal, presumably visual, memory strategy could be quite effective.  Perhaps when there is a delay, however, during which the blocks are covered, a verbal memory strategy becomes necessary for efficient performance.

(iii) Speech coding in memory.  There is another series of experiments which from a quite distinct starting point have examined the idea that retarded readers are deficient in the use of inner speech or phonological memory coding.  This idea has recently been advanced by I.Y. Liberman and her colleagues.  Liberman et al. (1977) used a procedure devised by Conrad (1964) for demonstrating phonological STM coding in adults.  This is to compare recall of visually presented strings of consonants which are similar to dis-similar in sound (rhyming or non-rhyming).  Conrad showed that fewer rhyming consonants were recalled even though they were presented visually.  Memory errors also corre-lated with the confusions made when listening for consonants in noise.  From this it was concluded that subjects were remembering the letters by their names.

Liberman et al. (1977) compared the recall of visually pre-sented rhyming and non-rhyming consonant strings in normal and retarded readers.  They found that while normal readers recalled fewer rhyming consonants the retarded readers recalled a similar number of the two types and also overall recalled fewer consonants.  Mark, Shankweiler, Liberman and Fowler (1977) showed that the same pattern was true for the recognition of words that had been read.  They concluded that the retarded readers were deficient in phonological memory coding.

There is a problem with this interpretation, which arises from experiments on auditory perception and memory in these groups.  Bradley and Bryant (1978) have shown that retar-ded readers have great difficulty in perceiving the similari-ties between rhyming words which they hear.  Shankweiler and Liberman (1976) report an auditory analogue of their letter memory test, comparing memory for sequences of rhyming and non-rhyming consonants.  Here retarded readers again remembered a similar number of the two letter types while the normal readers were worse on the rhyming letters.  Mark et al. (1977) discussing this experiment conclude 'that the nature of the poor readers' deficit is related to accessing and use of a phonetic representation regardless of the source of the linguistic information.'

Bradley and Bryant's results suggest a different interpretation. This is that the retarded readers may not differ in their ability or propensity to access a phonological memory code but that this code is different in these children in so far as they are not sensitive to the similarities between speech sounds. Mark et al. seem to be suggesting that even when retarded readers listen to strings of letters they do not remember them in a speech like form (how else can they do this task?). From these results, however, an equally likely explanation is that although they may use a phonological memory code in these experiments their performance is less affected by similarities between the sounds of the items which they remember.

There is one other experiment which suggests that retarded readers may rely less on phonological memory than normal readers. Spring and Capps (1974) proposed that the naming difficulties of this group may reduce their ability to use a phonological code and this may generally discourage them from using such a strategy. In their experiment they compared a group of retarded readers with a group of normal readers. Naming speed was measured by the time taken to name sequences of digits, colours, and drawings of objects, as quickly as possible. The retarded readers were slow at naming, as others have found (Denckla and Rudel, 1976; Audley, 1976).

Following the naming test a probed recall task was given. Eight cards each presenting one of the digits 1-8 were shown to the subject and placed face down in front of them. A probe digit was then presented and the subject was asked to point to the card with the matching digit. As well as recording responses, the experimenter observed the subject's eye movements. Two groups were identified, subjects who typically moved their eyes from left to right stopping at the card of their choice were labelled scanners, all others were classified as non-scanners. A pilot study with adults had shown that they typically performed as scanners. This was interpreted as indicative of the use of cumulative verbal rehearsal; the subjects scanning forward as they recite the digits in the rehearsed order.

One out of the 24 control children were non-scanners, as compared to 11 out of the 24 retarded readers. This was interpreted as showing a lack of cumulative rehearsal in the

retarded readers. Probed recall differed between these
groups in a manner which was consistent with this. Scanners showed the typical serial position curve with recall
of early and late items being more likely than those in the
middle of the list. Non-scanners showed no primacy effect
but a normal recency effect. This is consistent with the
idea that these subjects were deficient in their use of cumulative rehearsal given the commonly held view that primacy
effects reflect the cumulative rehearsal of early items. The
retarded readers remembered the digits less well than the
controls.

These experiments by Spring and Capps, and also those
by the Liberman group, are further evidence for poor short
term verbal memory in retarded readers. The Spring and
Capps study provides evidence that the deficit in memory for
visually presented verbal items reflects a reluctance to
recode these items into a speech-like form, or perhaps a
reluctance to rehearse the items once they are so recoded.
The results of the Liberman group have also been interpreted in this way but according to the arguments advanced
here such an interpretation is not a necessary conclusion
from these studies. An alternative is that retarded readers
are simply less sensitive to the similarities between speech
sounds.

The idea that retarded readers tend not to rely on a speech
code in these short term memory tasks implies that they rely
on some alternative, presumably visual, memory strategy.
Direct evidence for this possibility is lacking. One suggestive piece of evidence supports this idea. As described
earlier (p. 26), Stanley (1976) found that retarded
readers were better than controls at identifying briefly presented masked digits when the response was to press a
labelled button. Furthermore it is reported that the retarded readers made consistent errors by confusing digits with
curved features, suggesting they were relying on making
direct visual matches in this situation, while the normal
readers did not exhibit any such stable pattern. This is a
potentially important result deserving further study, since
it suggests that the use of an alternative visual processing
strategy characterises this group, and that this may actually
result in better performance on some tasks.

(iv) Long term verbal memory. All these studies have
been concerned with short term memory processes. There
are many clinical reports of poor long term verbal memory
in retarded readers. For example, teachers often comment

on their difficulty remembering arbitrary sequences such as days of the week, and months of the year and their word finding difficulties (for a description of such a case see Bradley, Hulme and Bryant (1979)).   Spring and Capps (1974) and Denckla and Rudel (1976) have demonstrated these word finding difficulties experimentally by showing that these children are slow at naming common objects, digits and colours.   This is evidence for poor retrieval from long term verbal memory in these children.   Surprisingly, there are almost no experimental studies of long term memory in these children.

The only studies which fall into this category are paired associate learning studies.   These have already been described in the discussion of cross-modal abilities.   To recap on these findings, retarded readers show consistently poor performance on PAL tasks involving a verbal component (Gascon and Goodglass, 1970; Vellutino, Steger, Harding and Phillips, 1975; Vellutino, Bentley and Phillips, 1978; Rudel, Denckla and Spalten, 1976).   In non-verbal tasks they perform within normal limits equally consistently, irrespective of the modality or combination of modalities involved (Goyen and Lyle, 1971b; Vellutino, Steger and Pruzek, 1973; Vellutino, Harding, Phillips and Steger, 1975; Vellutino, Steger, Harding and Phillips, 1975; Steger, Vellutino and Meshoulam, 1972).   It seems that the difficulties manifested by these children in remembering verbal materials for a short time are parallelled in these few studies of long term memory.   More studies in this area are badly needed.   The interesting possibility remains that they may have even greater difficulty remembering verbal materials over extended time periods comparable to those involved in learning to read, than for short periods as assessed by nearly all the experiments investigating their abilities.


SUMMARY AND CONCLUSIONS

It is clear that a substantial number of children, probably as many as 4 per cent, experience significant difficulties in learning to read in spite of having adequate intelligence and normal sensory abilities and receiving conventional instruction.   In this chapter some of the characteristics of these children have been reviewed and a special emphasis has been placed on the problem of demonstrating the causes of their reading problems. Very little can be said with any certainty on this complex issue but at least the appropriate questions to ask are now becoming clear.

In considering the possible general causes of reading retardation it seems likely that the difficulties of these children are in part biologically determined. There is suggestive evidence of a genetic influence operating and other evidence of an association with birth hazards which are likely causes of minor brain damage. When examined by neurologists these children rarely show frank abnormalities, but often show evidence of cerebral immaturity in tests of language and motor skills.

At the same time it is obvious that reading is a skill that must be taught and language skills which are involved in learning to read are sensitive to the stimulation provided by the child's environment. It is clear that any biological predisposition to reading difficulties will be exacerbated by these influences. Furthermore, to say that these children's difficulties may depend partly upon their constitutional make-up is not to diminish in any way the importance of remedial teaching to help them learn to read.

The importance of psychological research into the cognitive mechanisms underlying these children's reading problems lies in the hope it provides for improving such teaching, as well as in possibly increasing our understanding of reading processes and learning to read in general. Certain weaknesses in design severely limit the conclusions which can be drawn from many of these studies. In particular the habit of ignoring the ambiguities of correlational findings and the widespread, if implicit, assumption of a unique cause for all cases of reading retardation, seem particularly damaging.

The problem of interpreting correlational findings becomes acute in the light of evidence for a general immaturity of the central nervous system in these children. This makes it likely that their performance will differ from that of normals on many psychological tasks, but many of these differences may be reflections of this immaturity which are not causally related to the reading problem. Because of this, the possible logical connections between difficulties on experimental tasks and the reading process must be scrutinised carefully.

In considering the varieties of reading retardation it seems probable that at least two types of cause will be necessary to explain all cases. A likely cause for the majority of cases is some form of language impairment and verbal learning difficulty; there may also be another smaller group, however, for whom a visual memory impairment is the problem, and perhaps other children experience both sorts of difficulties.

Experiments examining these issues have generally compared groups of retarded and normal readers on various perceptual and memory tasks thought to be relevant to reading. Findings on the visual perceptual and memory abilities of this group are often contradictory but there is no good evidence for a general deficit amongst these children in this sphere. Most importantly, the experiments whose visual requirements are most similar to reading, but where verbal skills are not required, show no differences between retarded and normal readers. These reports of mean differences may, however, conceal a small sub-group of retarded readers, for whom such problems are important.

On the other hand, the oral language and verbal memory skills of retarded readers as a group are shown to be consistently worse than those of controls in this type of study. The idea of a cross-modal deficit in these children appears to be more or less conclusively ruled out by present evidence, but these experiments do provide a further demonstration of their language difficulties.

The first experiments reported here will make a further exploration of the memory abilities of retarded readers, since this approach seems to hold considerable promise for understanding these children's problems. A comparison will be made between the same groups of retarded and normal readers on tests of verbal and visual memory. On the basis of the research reviewed in this chapter it seems likely that most retarded readers do not sustain a basic deficit of visual memory. It remains a strong possibility, however, that a sub-group of these children does have such problems. The retarded readers' performance on the visual memory task will be examined for evidence of this possible sub-group.

In contrast to this expectation of normal performance on a test of visual memory, it seems likely that the retarded readers will be worse than normals on a test of verbal memory. If such a deficit is revealed in an initial comparison between groups of normal and retarded readers matched for age and IQ, it will be explored further in a comparison with controls matched for reading age. In this way it is hoped to assess the likelihood of such differences being a cause of the reading problem.

In addition to these questions, a major aim of the present

work is to explore some methods of remedial teaching which reputedly help retarded readers learn to read.   In these methods they trace around words as if writing them with their finger-tip, while learning to read.   Although these so called multi-sensory methods are widely used, formal evidence for their effectiveness is scarce, and we understand little about the possible mechanisms involved.   A further question is how these mechanisms might relate to the retarded readers' cognitive deficits.   It is to a consideration of these multi-sensory teaching methods that we now turn.

# 2 Multi-sensory teaching: tracing as a teaching aid for retarded readers

BACKGROUND IN EDUCATIONAL PRACTICE

The ideas dealt with in Chapter 1 about the nature of the retarded reader's difficulties came largely from psychologists and neurologists. In this chapter we now turn to consider certain ideas from the field of education about how retarded readers may be helped to learn to read. These ideas have largely been ignored by psychologists, however. This seems a pity. It will be argued that research into these ideas is important for at least two reasons. Most directly it may help to improve these teaching procedures. Second, it may improve our understanding of the origin of the retarded reader's difficulties. If these methods help retarded readers learn to read and write, when they have failed to do so by more conventional methods, an understanding of why this is so could clarify the nature of their original learning difficulties.

One of the most consistent and specific suggestions about teaching these children concerns the role of writing movements, the idea being that emphasis on the movements made while writing, or more particularly on the movements made while tracing around words as if writing them, may help these children learn to read. These teaching methods are often called multi-sensory because they entail input from the different sense modalities involved in tracing, saying and seeing the word which is being learnt.

These ideas originate with Grace M. Fernald (1943; Fernald and Keller, 1921). She advocated that children with reading difficulties be taught to read and write each word as and when it occurred as part of their desire to express themselves in written work with their teacher. The word was

written out in large, cursive script by the teacher, and the
child then traced it with finger contact saying each syllable
as it was traced.   After each tracing, the child tried to
write the word without copying, if a mistake occurred it
was not corrected;  it was abandoned and a fresh attempt
made.   This procedure was repeated until the child could
write the word from memory.

It is clear from Fernald's description, with its stress on
the smooth completion of attempts to write the word without
copying, that she considered memory for the movements
made while tracing the word to be important.   She did not
have a more elaborate or explicit theory of how the method
worked than this, although Fernald and Keller (1921) talk of
kinaesthetic cues from tracing and pronouncing the word
linking its spoken and written forms.

Orton (1928) also recommended the use of tracing in
teaching children with reading difficulties, and linked this
to his ideas about directional confusion and incomplete
laterality as the sources of reading difficulties.   To quote
from his article:

If confusion in the direction of reading forms the obstacle
to proper association of the printed word with its meaning, the obvious corrective measures should be aimed at
training for consistent direction in reading.... One very
valuable aid immediately suggests itself here, and that is
the inclusion of kinaesthetic directional training in the
building up of associations.   In general the reeducation
methods which we propose may be said to be based on
training for simultaneous association of visual, auditory
and kinaesthetic fields, i.e., tracing and sounding the
visually presented word and maintaining consistent direction by following the letters with the finger during sound
synthesis of syllables and words.

Following Orton, and working with him, Gillingham and
Stillman (1956) developed a method of teaching for retarded
readers based on tracing.   The major difference between
this and Fernald's method was its greater emphasis on
phonics and its more systematic approach.

The source of these methods was almost certainly the
work of Montessori (1915).   She advocated that young
children should begin learning to write before learning to
read and recommended the finger tracing of sandpaper cut-
outs of letters as a pre-reading exercise.   Another of her
procedures was the use of sand trays for the practice of
writing movements with the fingers.   Much more distantly,

Quintilian in AD 68 apparently recommended teaching children to read by having them trace words cut out of wood (Haarhoof, 1920).

These methods clearly have a long history in educational practice. They are still used by the teachers of these children and are recommended by experienced remedial teachers (Cotterell, 1970b; Wolff, 1970). A major aim of the experiments reported here is to obtain evidence about how and why such methods work - if they do.


## THE EFFECTIVENESS OF THESE METHODS

Formal evidence for the effectiveness of tracing as a teaching aid in cases of reading retardation is scarce. The little evidence there is has not penetrated into the general literature on reading, as witnessed by the scant attention given to this question in Gibson and Levin's (1975) recent and comprehensive book, 'The Psychology of Reading'.

Fernald (1943; Fernald and Keller, 1921) quotes case histories where there were dramatic improvements in the reading of severely retarded readers when they were taught by her methods. Orton (1928) refers very briefly to the success with which tracing had been used to teach retarded readers in his clinic. Cynics might quickly dismiss these reports on two counts. Insufficient detail of the procedures and subjects are given and no controls were included. Even if it is accepted that some children were helped in such programmes, other uncontrolled factors in the teaching situation which had nothing to do with tracing might account for the improvements.

Interest in these methods in the educational literature has been spasmodic and fragmentary. There are a few more controlled studies of the effects of tracing on the teaching of reading, but these often leave a lot to be desired in terms of their methodology and reporting.

In the first, Kirk (1933) studied the effects of tracing on teaching six mentally sub-normal boys to read single words. Two groups of randomly selected three-letter words were taught to each boy. One group of words was taught by having the child look at and say the word; for the other group they also traced around each word. The presentation time for each word was held constant. The experiment lasted for several days. The teaching method alternated across days and the order of these methods was balanced across subjects. The trials to learn each set of five words presented on one day was the same for each method. Retention was measured by testing the reading of each set of five words on the day after it had been learnt and by the number of trials required to relearn each list. On both these measures all six boys showed better performance after having traced the words. The procedure of this experiment seems adequate. Interpretation is complicated, however, by the use of a small sample of mentally subnormal subjects.

Pulliam (1945) investigated the effects of tracing around words formed by indentations in heavy card on learning to read them. The addition of this tactile component presumably derives from the influence of Montessori's work. Each child was given two word lists to read, the words on each list being matched to equate them for difficulty and configuration. Each pupil was taught over a period of two weeks an equal number of words from the two lists which he had not been able to read. One set was taught by tracing the indented word cards, the other by a look and say method with the words typed on cards. The same teacher did all the teaching. Each child was taught for ten minutes a day and during this time four words were taught. The order of teaching methods was counterbalanced across children, each method it appears being used for one day at a time. Two weeks after the end of this teaching programme the children were given the two word lists to read again. A mixed group of eighteen children were seen in the study. Six were 'seriously retarded in reading', four were 'slow' and the other eight were 'making normal progress'; all were of normal intelligence.

The results showed that more of the words taught by tracing were correctly read by the children, and no differences were reported between the normal and retarded readers. Every child in fact read more of the words that had been traced. No statistical treatment of these results is given.

Again there are problems with this study. The word list taught by the tracing method was slightly easier, in that fewer words on this list were misread in the initial testing. The final results are only presented, however, as the total percentage correctly read on each list at the completion of teaching. This would have been unequal before any teaching had taken place. Even so, the differences reported are large; 89.5 per cent of words on the traced list were read compared with 44.5 per cent on the non-traced list.

Another complicating factor is the use of physically different words for teaching in the two conditions. Indented word cards were used to teach the words which were traced around, while conventional typed words were used for the look and say condition. The indented word cards may have been visually more salient and distinctive and easier to remember than the typed words. This seems unlikely, and final testing appears to have been done with conventional typed material in both cases, but this possibility cannot be ruled out.

A third study which has also reported favourably on the use of tracing as a remedial teaching aid is that of Talmadge, Davids and Laufer (1963). This study is, however, even less satisfactory than the previous ones. Here twenty-four children were seen. All were emotionally disturbed and at least two years retarded in reading, and fourteen of them showed signs of brain damage. Half the children were assigned to a control group which was taught by 'traditional methods', and half were taught by a method which incorporated tracing. This was not the only aid used, however. A complex programme including much writing practice in sand and clay and on blackboards was used. Emphasis was given to phonics. The children also played with three-dimensional block letters and rapid exposures of words that they were learning to read. The same teachers taught reading to both groups for one hour a day, for three months.

At the end of the three month period, the experimental group had made more progress with reading than the controls. These were only small groups, however, and no statistical treatment of the results are given. Furthermore, it is not clear whether the use of tracing activities with the experimental group of children was responsible for any difference or whether other complex differences in the teaching procedures used were responsible.

Thus, these three studies all give some support to the use of tracing as a teaching aid for retarded readers, although they are all inadequate in some respects. One study, however, has challenged the use of these techniques. Jensen and King (1970) found that tracing around words did not lead to them being read better. In this study the subjects were normal 4- and 5-year-old kindergarten children. This makes any results of the study less than directly relevant to whether or not such procedures can help retarded readers, because here only young children of average ability were studied. A further objection to this study lies in its method. The authors viewed tracing as a means of discrimination training to help the young child distinguish between similar words. The reason for this view is obscure in the absence of any evidence for visual discrimination problems being a limiting factor in learning to read. Whatever the reason, this led to using the tracing procedure before the child read the word. Each word was traced, then removed, and the child asked to read a separate exemplar of it. However, both Fernald and Gillingham and Stillman stressed that tracing and saying the word should be performed simultaneously. The fact that this study ignored this point may have been responsible for the absence of any effect of tracing. In addition, it is quite possible that a method which helps older retarded readers may not be of benefit to young normal children.

In conclusion there is very limited evidence from these experimental studies that tracing is an effective remedial teaching procedure for retarded readers. In addition to these limited experimental findings, however, we must take seriously the considerable faith among the teachers of these children that these methods do work. There is certainly enough evidence favouring these methods to justify further studies of them.


MECHANISMS UNDERLYING THESE METHODS

Let us accept for the moment that tracing does help retarded readers learn to read and write. Why might this be so? A few studies have addressed this question and their findings may also be relevant to whether these methods are effective or not. Most of these studies have been concerned with the possible effects of tracing on visual perception and memory. This emphasis is presumably derived from the many attempts to explain reading retardation in these terms.

A common idea has been that tracing may help retarded readers by improving their ability to discriminate between letters and words. As mentioned before this was the idea in the Jensen and King study which led them to ignore a possibly important aspect of these teaching procedures. A large problem for these studies is that, as we have seen in Chapter 1, there is no good evidence that visual discrimination problems are a cause of reading retardation. Furthermore, Fernald certainly did not suggest that her method was effective because of its effects on visual discrimination

abilities.   It is perhaps not surprising that research which
has taken this approach has not produced encouraging
results.

There are two studies apart from the Jensen and King
study (mentioned in the last section) which fall into this
category.   In one, Levin, Watson and Feldman (1964), used
tracing as a pre-training exercise with 6-year-old average
readers.   Their task was to learn to associate names with
strings of abstract shapes.   Different groups traced different parts of the strings of shapes before the paired associate training began.   Tracing did not improve PAL performance; which is in agreement with the Jensen and King study
using a conventional reading task.

In the second, Williams (1975) examined more directly
whether tracing improved visual discrimination abilities in
normal 4- and 5-year-olds.   She compared the effects of
training on a copying and a matching to sample task on tests
of these abilities with letter-like forms as stimuli.   The
training had highly specific effects.   Training in copying
improved the ability to copy, and training in matching
improved scores on a matching test.

These negative results certainly do not show tracing to be
an ineffective teaching aid for retarded readers, because
they deal only with the effects of tracing in young normal
children.   What they do indicate is that for these subjects
tracing does not improve reading by improving the discrimination of letter and word forms.   This is not surprising.
There is no good evidence that problems in discriminating
visual forms are ever the limiting factor in the learning of
normal or retarded readers.   In this light, it is hard to
see whey these studies started from this position.

A far more reasonable approach is to look at the possible
effects of tracing on memory, since it seems likely from the
evidence dealt with in Chapter 1 that reading retardation
may depend in part upon some form of verbal memory deficiency.   Several studies have looked at the effects of tracing upon memory for verbal materials in retarded readers.
The results of these studies are much more encouraging.

The first of these studies was by Berman (1939).   The
subjects for the first experiment were seventeen children of
average intelligence who were retarded in reading by at
least two years.   Their task was to learn to recognise a
set of nonsense syllables.   Two teaching methods were
used; in one the subject looked at and said the syllable, in
the other he also simultaneously traced it.   Both methods

were used with all children. The order of the methods was counterbalanced across subjects; half traced first while the other half used the look and say method first. The same syllables were taught by the two methods on alternate days.

The memory test required subjects to recognise the syllables from among sets of similar ones presented on a card. Two measures were taken. One of these was the number of trials necessary for the correct recognition of all the five syllables presented in one session, and the other measure was the number correctly recognised the following day. The results showed that tracing improved immediate recognition by 8 per cent but did not improve delayed recognition.

In a second experiment the method was essentially identical except for the use of abstract geometric shapes. Here tracing again improved immediate recognition, this time by 19 per cent, but again it did not improve delayed recognition.

In the next study of this problem Forster (1941) had psychology undergraduates learn to read words represented by a complex novel script in which there was a regular correspondence between the script symbols and the phonic elements of the words. Tracing did not aid learning to read this new script; on the contrary, it hindered it. This experiment is not really relevant to assessing the use of tracing as a teaching aid for retarded readers because of the highly sophisticated subjects involved. Furthermore, it appears that for these subjects the task was really one of code breaking. They could perform this task best by working out the correspondence between the script symbols and the sounds in the spoken words paired with them. One would not expect tracing to aid such conceptual learning. The result that tracing hindered such learning reflects the fact that it probably distracted subjects from this task.

Roberts and Coleman (1958) looked at the effects of tracing in a group of retarded readers and a group of normal readers learning to write nonsense syllables. Twenty nonsense syllables were taught by having each child either look at, or look and trace, each syllable. The order of these conditions being balanced within each group.

During each session the child was shown a series of five nonsense syllables which were either looked at or looked at and traced. After each presentation the child tried to write the five syllables from memory. Trials to achieve correct reproduction of all five was the measure of learning used. The retarded readers learned the nonsense syllables in fewer trials when they were traced but no such improvement was found for the normal readers. In addition the control group learned the nonsense syllables quicker than the retarded readers in the visual presentation condition. Thus it appears that for retarded readers tracing aids memory for verbal materials, but that it is not so effective for children of average ability.

Roberts and Coleman interpreted their results in terms of a visual memory failure in the retarded readers which was attenuated by tracing. They also administered a test of visual perception and found that the retarded readers were worse on this than controls. This result conflicts, however, with the large body of work reviewed in Chapter 1, on the visual perceptual abilities of retarded readers. Imperfections in the matching of the retarded and normal readers on IQ (there was a mean difference of seven IQ points between the groups) may have been responsible for this difference. The other obvious criticism of this conclusion is that learning to write a series of nonsense syllables from memory is primarily a verbal and not a visual memory task. There is good evidence that when normal adult subjects are presented with visual letter sequences to memorise they do so by means of a speech-like memory code (e.g., Conrad, 1964). By extrapolation it seems certain that the strategy adopted by subjects required to memorise a series of nonsense syllables would be to remember them in a speechlike form also. This explanation also explains the poor performance of the retarded readers on this task. As we saw in Chapter 1, there is good evidence that they are poor on various tests of verbal memory while there is no adequate evidence that as a group they are poor on tests of visual non-verbal memory.

One other study has also found that tracing improves memory for nonsense syllables amongst retarded readers. Ofman and Shaevitz (1963) had three groups of ten retarded readers learn a series of ten nonsense syllables. One group looked at and said the nonsense syllables, another group also traced each nonsense syllable with his finger tip while saying it, and a third group traced the syllables by following its outline with his eyes. Memory was measured by the number of nonsense syllables that were correctly written to dictation after the lists of syllables had been presented three times.

The results showed that the eye and finger tracing groups did not differ from each other and that both wrote more of the syllables correctly than the control group. Ofman and

Shaevitz suggest that this result indicates that tracing's
beneficial effects on memory are due to its attention directing properties.   The logic behind this is obscure.   Tracing
something with one's eyes involves movement just as tracing
something with one's finger does.   There is another major
problem in interpreting this study which is the small size of
the groups studied.   This is especially critical since no
details of the different groups' IQs are given.   Nevertheless, it is of interest that manual tracing again had a beneficial effect here as in the other two studies where verbal
materials were presented to retarded readers.


## SUMMARY AND CONCLUSIONS

One of the most consistent and specific ideas which has been
applied to the problem of teaching retarded readers is to
have them manually trace around the words they are learning
to read.   More broadly, emphasis is often put on teaching
them to read by having them write.   Although such methods
are widely used, and are favoured by the teachers of retarded readers, formal evidence for their effectiveness is
scarce.   The few studies to date suffer from various inadequacies but they are fairly consistent in providing support
for these methods.
   If such evidence is accepted for the moment, the further
question is raised as to why such methods should work.
Hopefully an answer to this would also throw further light
on the nature of the causes of reading retardation.   A few
studies have looked at this further question.   Some have
been guided by the idea that tracing may help the child to
visually discriminate between similar words.   The results
of these, all with normal children as subjects, have been
negative.   Results such as this, derived from studies of
normal children, must be treated with caution when considering the use of these methods with retarded readers.   This
approach to understanding these methods does not seem a
promising one, however.   Advocates of these methods have
not suggested they work in this way, and there is no evidence that retarded readers experience difficulties in
making visual discriminations between letters and words.
   A better line of research has been to explore whether
tracing improves memory for written verbal material amongst
retarded readers.   There is reasonable evidence from three
studies that this is so, and it also appears to be true of
memory for abstract geometric shapes.

Our understanding of this effect of tracing on the retarded readers' memory for written language is very poor. One suggestion is that it is an attentional effect. The experimental support for this is inadequate, however. In any case, this seems too simple an explanation. If this is all that tracing does, why have the teachers of retarded readers not employed a variety of other attention-directing ploys? It seems hard to believe from experience with retarded readers that a simple lack of attention is the block to their acquisition of reading skills.

Another explanation for the effects of tracing upon the retarded readers' memory for nonsense syllables is in terms of poor visual memory abilities. There are two major objections to this explanation. Memory for these materials is more likely to depend upon verbal memory abilities, and there is no evidence that poor visual memory is a characteristic of most retarded readers.

One final gap in this research is that there is no evidence that tracing can aid memory in normal readers. The one study to have examined this is that of Roberts and Coleman, and they found a non-significant effect of tracing on memory for nonsense syllables amongst normal readers. It would be surprising if the effects of tracing on memory for graphic forms were completely restricted to retarded readers. A confirmation of the fact that normal readers do not benefit from tracing verbal materials when memorising them, and a demonstration of the circumstances (if any) under which their memory is improved by tracing, would improve our understanding of this effect and perhaps of the nature of the retarded readers' problems. It is to these questions that the first experiments reported here are directed.

# 3 The effects of tracing on memory for verbal and visual stimuli in retarded and normal readers

EXPERIMENT 1.  THE EFFECTS OF TRACING ON
MEMORY FOR LETTER SEQUENCES IN RETARDED AND
NORMAL READERS

Introduction

In this first experiment several of the questions which have
been raised in Chapters 1 and 2 will be examined by means
of a study of the effects of tracing on memory for letter
sequences in retarded and normal readers.   The first point
of interest is the efficiency of verbal memory processes in
these two groups.   According to much previous research
(see pp. 45–52) retarded readers are characterised by their
poor verbal memory abilities.   In the present experiments
memory for letter sequences is examined.   It is to be
expected, therefore, that retarded readers will perform
more poorly on this verbal memory task than normal readers.
   A second major issue is the effect of tracing on memory
for verbal materials.   According to previous experiments
(pp. 62–5) this ought to be facilitated in retarded readers.
Its possible effects in normal readers is less certain.
Roberts and Coleman (1958) found a much smaller effect of
tracing on learning to write nonsense syllables in normal
than in retarded readers, but no statistical assessment of
this difference between the groups was made.   This possible difference between normal and retarded readers will
be explored here.   The method employed in the present
experiment is a recognition memory procedure with random
letter strings.   This is simpler than the procedures in
previous experiments where the effects of tracing on learning to read or to write nonsense syllables have been

examined. Any positive results in the present experiment will provide evidence for the generality of the effects of tracing on memory.

The serial memory task used here also allows separate estimates of item and order memory to be made. In this way it is hoped to provide further evidence relevant to the idea that retarded readers may be particularly poor at remembering order information (pp. 46-9). This separation of item and order memory may also be relevant to assessing any effects of tracing on memory.

A final subsidiary question considered here is the use of three-dimension (3D) letters and their possible effects on memory. This question, which does not seem to have been examined experimentally before, is considered here because of teaching procedures. There have been suggestions from teachers that the use of 3D letters may be helpful in the remedial teaching of retarded readers. For example, one of the procedures incorporated in the study of Talmadge et al., referred to earlier, was to allow the retarded readers to handle 3D wooden letters. These procedures again almost certainly derive from the work of Montessori (1915) who gave young children such letters to handle in the early stages of reading instruction.

The only previous experimental studies which appear at all relevant to this question are concerned with discrimination learning. Several studies have found that children learn to discriminate 3D stimuli more quickly than 2D stimuli (e.g. Stevenson and McBee, 1958; Etaugh, 1970). In the light of this and the teaching procedures, it seemed reasonable to examine whether there were differences in memory for 2D and 3D letters in normal and retarded readers. If, for example, there were certain difficulties in visual memory amongst retarded readers, the use of 3D letters might be beneficial to them in a memory task.

Method

(a) Subjects. Twenty children of normal reading ability, and twenty retarded readers matched for age and IQ, participated in the experiment. Thirteen of the controls were boys, and seven girls; sixteen of the poor readers were boys and four were girls.

The preliminary selection of children for these two groups was made by consultation with their class teachers. In order to obtain the retarded readers the teachers were asked to refer any children who, in spite of being generally bright, had a severe and specific difficulty with reading. The normal readers were selected by asking the teachers for children whose reading level was near to, or slightly above, that expected on the basis of their age. Children selected in this way were then administered the Weschler Intelligence Scale for Children (WISC), and the Neale Analysis of Reading Ability. (The WISC is an individually administered IQ test which does not involve reading; the Neale Analysis of Reading Ability is an individually administered prose reading test.) The final decision to include or exclude each child was made on the basis of these test scores.

All controls were reading near to or above their age norms while the retarded readers had to be at least one year retarded in reading to be included and most were considerably more retarded than this. Details of the two groups are shown in Table 1.

TABLE 1 Details of the age, IQ, and reading levels of the normal and retarded readers who participated in Experiment 1

|  | Normal readers | Retarded readers | t | p |
|---|---|---|---|---|
| N | 20 | 20 |  |  |
| IQ (WISC) | 107.7 | 108.2 | 0.19 | N.S. |
| Age | 10 yr 3 mth | 10 yr 2 mth | 0.51 | N.S. |
| Reading age (Neale) | 11 yr 2 mth | 8 yr 1 mth | 8.71 | $p < 0.001$ |

(b) Design. A short term memory task was used. On each trial the subject attempted to remember, in order, a series of six or eight letters. Two types of letters were used, 2D or 3D, and there were two forms of presentation, visual (V) and visual plus tracing (VT). This gave four experimental conditions: 2D-V, 2D-VT, 3D-V, 3D-VT. In each condition there were three trials: one row of six letters followed by two rows of eight letters were presented. Each subject participated in all four conditions, the order of these being counterbalanced across subjects according to a Latin Square. The stimuli were counterbalanced across conditions.

(c) Materials. The materials consisted of two sets of the

fourteen consonants:  b, c, d, f, g, h, m, n, p, q, r, t, v,
w.    The 3D set consisted of commercially available coloured
plastic letters (Alpha–Beta–Set script letters).    The 2D
letters were copies of these plastic letters drawn in the
centre of 7.5 x 12.5 cm white cards, and coloured in ink to
match the 3D letters.    Each of these cards was protected by
a plastic cover.    All letter strings were random sets drawn
without replacement from the set of fourteen.

(d)  Procedure.    Testing was conducted in the subjects'
schools, either in a private room or a bay off the main
classroom depending on a particular school's facilities.
During testing the experimenter sat beside the subject at a
table divided by a large screen.    This enabled the experimenter to manipulate materials and record responses out of
the subject's sight.

The experiment was presented as a 'remembering game'.
An initial trial involving memory for three letters, which
was not scored, served to familiarise the subject with the
procedure and to check that the task was properly understood.    Similarly, before the first trial involving tracing,
this was demonstrated and practised by the subject.

A recognition/reconstruction procedure was used, in
which a letter string was displayed following which the
string was removed and the entire set of fourteen letters
were then laid out on the table in front of the subject.    Subjects then picked out the letters that were recognised and
arranged them to correspond to the order in which they had
been presented.    They were told always to pick out the
number of letters that had been presented even if this necessitated guessing.

On V trials a string of letters was laid out on the table in
front of the subject who then pointed to each letter in turn
and simultaneously said its name aloud.    Ample inspection
time was allowed.    The letters were then removed, and
shuffled together with the rest of the set, behind the screen.
The entire set was then laid out in random order in front of
the subject, for the recognition/reconstruction test.

The VT trials were essentially identical except that,
instead of pointing to each letter, subjects, watched by the
experimenter, traced around each in turn with their index
finger.    Care was taken to allow equal inspection time in
the V and VT conditions.    The time taken to shuffle the
letters was also held constant through the adoption of a
highly regular procedure.    The pointing and naming responses were used in an attempt to equate the general atten-

tiveness of subjects in the V and VT conditions and so
reduce the likelihood that any positive effects of tracing
could be attributed to attentional effects.


Results

(a) Method of scoring.  Separate measures of item and
order memory were used.  Item memory was simply measured by the number of correctly recognised letters on a
given trial irrespective of order.
  Scoring for order memory is less straightforward.
Commonly, measures based on the number of items recalled
in their correct serial position have been employed.  These
seem less than satisfactory for two reasons.  First, errors
in which sequences are transposed are penalised by such
procedures, despite the fact that they evidently reflect  hat
order information has been retained.
  The second problem with these measures is that they are
not independent of item memory.  Simply counting the number
of items in their correct serial position oviously confounds
item and order memory.  The common alternative is, therefore, to compute the proportion of correct items which are
also in their correct serial position.  Even this does not
constitute an independent measure of order memory, however.  As more items are recalled it becomes less likely
that by chance they will be recalled in their correct serial
positions.
  The measure of order memory used here overcomes both
these objections.  This is to calculate for each trial the
correlation (Kendall's tau) between the order in which correctly recognised items are arranged by the subject and the
order in which they were presented.  This measure gives
credit in cases where sequences are transposed, and is
also truly independent of the number of items recalled;
random arrangements will always be scored as zero irrespective of the number of items involved.
  (b) Item memory.  The means and standard deviations
for the number of letters correctly recognised in each of the
four conditions by the two groups of subjects are shown in
Table 2.
  There are several trends in these data that are of inter--
est.  Not surprisingly, in view of the previous evidence for
retarded readers having poor verbal memory abilities, the
retarded readers remember fewer letters than the normal

readers. The effect of tracing on memory seems generally beneficial. This seems to be more marked in the case of the retarded readers.

TABLE 2 Means and standard deviations for the number of letters correctly recognised by the two groups in each of the four conditions of Experiment 1

|  | 2D–V | 2D–VT | 3D–V | 3D–VT |
|---|---|---|---|---|
| Normal readers | 18.15 (1.90) | 18.65 (2.03) | 18.20 (1.70) | 18.30 (1.78) |
| Retarded readers | 16.35 (2.25) | 18.45 (1.67) | 17.00 (2.00) | 17.90 (1.97) |

(The maximum possible score in each condition is 22.)

The raw scores for letters correct were subjected to a 3-way (2 x 2 x 2) analysis of variance with reading ability a between subject variable, and presentation conditions (V or VT) and letter type (2D or 3D) within subject variables.

The three trends noted above were all statistically significant. The normal readers remembered more letters than the retarded readers ($F = 6.14$; d.f. 1, 38; $p < 0.025$) and tracing produced an improvement in memory ($F = 13.28$; d.f. 1, 38; $p < 0.001$). Most interestingly a significant interaction between groups and conditions showed that the effect of tracing varied between the normal and retarded readers ($F = 5.90$; d.f. 1, 38; $p < 0.025$). This interaction was explored using the Tukey HSD test. This showed that in the V condition the normal readers were significantly better than the retarded ($p < 0.05$) but that in the VT condition there was no significant difference between them; furthermore, tracing improved memory in the retarded ($p < 0.05$) but not in the normal readers.

The type of letters used (2D or 3D) had no significant effect on memory ($F < 1$; d.f. 1, 38; NS) and nor did any interaction with this factor approach significance.

(c) Order memory. Tau was calculated as a measure of order memory for each trial and averaged over trials in each condition for each subject. The means and standard deviations of these correlations for the two groups in each of the four conditions are shown in Table 3.

It appears that the normal readers remember the order of letters better than the retarded readers, and that tracing has a small but positive effect on memory for order.

TABLE 3 Means and standard deviations for the values of tau obtained by each of the groups in each condition in Experiment 1

|  | 2D–V | 2D–VT | 3D–V | 3D–VT |
| --- | --- | --- | --- | --- |
| Normal readers | 0.66 (0.249) | 0.70 (0.217) | 0.60 (0.313) | 0.63 (0.263) |
| Retarded readers | 0.49 (0.302) | 0.63 (0.283) | 0.58 (0.320) | 0.53 (0.350) |

These scores were subjected to an analysis of variance in the same way as the scores for items correct, with reading ability a between subject variable, and conditions (V or VT) and letter type (2D or 3D) within subject variables.

No effects in this analysis reached significance. In particular, neither the trend for the normal readers to remember the order of the letters better than the retarded readers ($F = 1.68$; d.f. 1, 38; NS) nor the trend for tracing to improve order memory ($F = 1.14$; d.f. 1, 38; NS) were significant. This contrasts with previous claims (see pp. 46-9) that retarded readers are particularly impaired in their memory for order.

The finding that these trends in the data were not significant in the analysis of variance was surprising. A possible reason for this appeared to be the large variance in the values of tau both across and within subjects. In order to counter possible criticisms that the large variance of tau was effectively swamping genuine effects in these data, further checks on the trends present were made by means of non-parametric tests.

The results of these tests essentially confirmed the findings of the analysis of variance. The difference in average correlations for each subject in the two groups was not significant (Mann Whitney; $U = 160.50$; NS). The largest difference between groups occurred in the 2D–V condition which is most comparable to the other experiments where differences in order memory for letters have been found between normal and retarded readers. This difference was barely significant in a Mann Whitney test ($U = 135.5$; $p < 0.05$; 1-tailed).

It appears therefore that even allowing for the greater variance of tau compared to other measures, the trend for normal readers to remember the order of letters better than retarded readers is less marked here than in other studies.

Discussion

(a) Item memory.  These results confirm that retarded
readers have difficulty in remembering series of letters
(e.g. Bakker, 1967; Liberman, Shankweiler, Liberman,
Fowler and Fischer, 1977) and in more general terms this
is consistent with their poor performance on a host of other
verbal memory tasks (see pp. 45-52).  These memory difficulties may in turn be considered as manifestations of an
underlying language impairment (see pp.

Perhaps the most interesting finding of the present experiment is that tracing should only improve memory for visually
presented letters in the retarded readers.  This is consistent with the Roberts and Coleman (1958) findings, where a
different test of memory was used.  The improvement in
memory for letters amongst the retarded readers following
tracing is also consistent with the other studies in this
field (see pp. 44-5).

In the present experiment the use of 3D letters had no
effects on memory in either the normal or retarded readers.
This seems to cast some doubt on the use of such letters in
remedial teaching, although obviously the present experiment differs in many ways from the teaching situation.  The
positive effects of 3D objects in visual discrimination learning studies, mentioned in the Introduction, do not appear to
generalise to a short-term verbal memory situation.

The fact that tracing improved memory for letters in
retarded but not in normal readers must now be considered.
A possible explanation for this comes from considering the
retarded readers' use of speech coding in memory.  It is
well known that adults in a similar situation to the present
experiment will remember a series of visually presented
letters by their names, even when this is inefficient because
the letter names are very similar, and so confusing
(Conrad, 1964; Conrad and Hull, 1964).  In current terminology they use a phonological memory code (i.e., a
speech based code whose form is acoustic, articulatory or
both).  It is plausible that both the differences in memory
for letters and the differential effects of tracing in normal
and retarded readers may depend on differences in the use
of such phonological memory codes.  The retarded readers
making less use of phonological coding, and by inference,
relying more on an alternative visual memory code.

This interpretation was suggested by informal observations of the children during the experiment.  The normal

readers showed more evidence of verbal rehearsal of the
letter names by mouthing them while waiting to perform the
recognition test than did the retarded readers. The normal
readers also more often picked out letters in their order of
presentation, suggesting the use of a rehearsed sequence of
names, while the retarded readers appeared to rely more on
a look and recognise procedure. This explanation is also
consistent with other evidence reviewed earlier (pp. 49–51)
which suggested that retarded readers are poor at using
phonological memory codes.

According to this view the retarded readers remember
fewer letters because their visual strategy is less efficient
than the normal readers' phonological one. The fact that
tracing only aids memory for letters in retarded readers
might also relate to their greater reliance on visual coding.
Perhaps tracing only improves memory for visual forms, not
for those remembered in terms of their names.

Experiment 2 was designed to test this explanation.

(b) Order memory. No particular predictions were made
concerning the effects of tracing on order memory. The
fact that tracing did not improve memory for order here is
at first surprising; the retarded reader's task is to learn
the sequence of letters composing words, and one would
expect that if tracing helps, it does so by aiding memory for
sequences of letters rather than just individual letters.
This paradox may reflect the fact that tracing as a teaching
aid is used in conjunction with words written in cursive
script while in the present experiment discrete letters were
used. If so, tracing cursive letter sequences should
improve memory for their order as well as for the individual
letters.

A surprising aspect of the present results is that the
retarded readers were not significantly worse than the good
readers in their memory for order. This contrasts with
several other studies which show that when retarded readers
are required to reconstruct the order of a sequence of items
(these being provided) they are worse at this than normals
(pp. 46–9). These studies can be criticised, however, for
the assumption that by providing the items and merely
requiring an ordering response, differences in item memory
are controlled. The retarded reader's difficulty in
remembering the items will still hamper memory for order
as assessed here. If items are forgotten you cannot by
definition remember their order.

The present method of calculating the correlation between

the order of correctly recognised items and their order of
presentation overcomes this difficulty, because here memory
for order is only assessed for items which are remembered.
It appears, therefore, that when a measure of order memory
which is truly independent of item memory is used, differences between normal and retarded readers are less marked.
It remains true, however, that the retarded readers were
consistently, though non-significantly, worse in their
memory for the order of the letters than were the normal
readers.

## EXPERIMENT 2. THE EFFECTS OF TRACING ON MEMORY FOR ABSTRACT FORMS IN RETARDED AND NORMAL READERS

### Introduction

In order to test the idea about phonological coding differences as an explanation of the results of Experiment 1, the
present experiment was conducted with the same groups of
children. This experiment is a non-verbal analogue of
Experiment 1, in which a set of abstract forms was used
instead of letters. If the pattern of results in Experiment
1 reflects differences in the use of phonological memory
codes between the groups, two predictions can be made
about performance on an equivalent non-verbal task. First,
overall levels of performance in the normal and retarded
readers should be the same if the retarded readers' memory
difficulties are purely verbal. Performance on such a non-
verbal visual memory task will also provide further evidence
relevant to the retarded readers visual memory abilities.
A second prediction concerns the effects of tracing on
memory in the two groups. It was hypothesised earlier
that the benefit afforded to the retarded readers in remembering the letters after tracing, reflected their reliance on
a visual memory code. If this is true, then in a non-verbal
task, where all subjects presumably must rely on visual
memory, tracing ought to be equally beneficial to both
groups.
   Both these predictions depend on the abstract forms being
treated as visual configurations and not being named.
Although it is impossible to ensure this, the forms are not
easy to name, and observations of the children memorising
them were certainly consistent with names not being used.

## Method

This experiment examined memory for non-verbal stimuli and was identical to Experiment 1, except for the differences described below.  The same children participated in both experiments and the order of experiments was counter-balanced across subjects in each group, i.e., half the children in each group performed Experiment 1 first, and half Experiment 2 first.

(a) Design.  A short term memory task of the same form as in Experiment 1 was used.  There were two experimental conditions; visual (V) and visual plus tracing (VT).  A demonstration trial involving memory for three forms, which was not scored, preceded each condition.  In each condition the subject was presented with two strings of six, and one string of eight forms to remember in order.  These strings were random sets drawn from the set of 14 without replacement.  The order of conditions was counterbalanced across subjects within each group.  The stimuli were counterbalanced across conditions.

(b) Materials.  The stimuli consisted of a set of fourteen abstract forms selected from those used by Gibson, Gibson, Pick and Osser (1962).  Each form was drawn in black ink in the centre of a 7.5 x 12.5 cm white card which was protected by a clear plastic cover.

(c) Procedure.  This was identical to Experiment 1, except that subjects could not name the forms as they had the letters.

## Results

The scoring of results was identical to Experiment 1.

(a) Item memory.  The means and standard deviations for the number of shapes correctly recognised by the two groups in each condition are shown in Table 4.

TABLE 4  Means and standard deviations for the number of forms correctly recognised by the two groups in each of the two conditions in Experiment 2

|  | V | VT |
| --- | --- | --- |
| Normal readers | 15.45 (2.164) | 17.50 (2.929) |
| Retarded readers | 14.65 (2.434) | 17.05 (2.395) |

(The maximum possible score in each condition is 20.)

Here the normal readers remember slightly more than the retarded readers but this difference is much smaller than in the case of the letters in Experiment 1.  Tracing again improves memory, but in this case, to a similar extent for the two groups.

The results were subjected to a 3-way (2 x 2 x 2) analysis of variance with presentation conditions (V or VT) as a within subject variable and order of presentation conditions, and reading ability as between subject variables.

This analysis revealed that tracing improved memory ($F = 24.22$; d.f. 1, 36; $p < 0.001$).  The only other significant result was the interaction between presentation conditions and their order ($F = 6.75$; d.f. 1, 36; $p < 0.025$).  A Tukey HSD test showed that tracing had a large and beneficial effect on memory when the VT condition was first ($p < 0.01$) but produced an insignificant improvement when this condition was second.  This probably reflects a simple decrease in performance over trials, but as in the present experiment order and stimuli are confounded this interpretation must remain tentative.  A decrease in performance over trials does seem a reasonable explanation for this result, however, since different combinations of the same set of forms were presented on successive trials.  In this situation we would expect the build up of proactive interference to cause a decrease in correct recognitions on later trials.

No other F ratios in this analysis exceeded 1.0.  It is particularly notable that the effects of reading ability did not approach significance ($F = < 1.0$; d.f. 1, 36; NS) showing that the retarded readers essentially remembered the shapes as well as the good readers.  The interaction between groups and presentation conditions was also absent in this case ($F = < 1.0$; d.f. 1, 36; NS) confirming that here tracing was equally beneficial to memory in both groups.

(b) Order memory.  The means and standard deviations of the correlations for each group in the two conditions are shown in Table 5.

TABLE 5  Means and standard deviations for the values of tau obtained by each group in each condition in Experiment 2

|                  | V             | VT            |
|------------------|---------------|---------------|
| Normal readers   | 0.58 (0.281)  | 0.68 (0.232)  |
| Retarded readers | 0.52 (0.279)  | 0.55 (0.287)  |

As in Experiment 1, the differences between these correlations are small. The retarded readers again appear slightly worse at remembering order and tracing again leads to a slight improvement in order memory.

The correlations were subjected to an analysis of variance in the same way as the scores for items correct, with presentation conditions (V or VT) as a within subject variable and order of presentation conditions and reading ability as between subject variables.

No effects in this analysis were significant. The normal and retarded readers did not differ in their ability to remember the order of the shapes ($F = 1.95$; d.f. 1, 36; NS) and tracing did not significantly improve order memory ($F = 1.61$; d.f. 1, 36; NS).

To check that genuine effects in these data were not being obscured by the large variance of the values of tau, the trends here were again examined by means of Mann Whitney U Tests. These confirmed the findings of the analysis of variance. No significant effects were found. Tracing did not reliably improve order memory in either group (normal readers $U = 148$ NS; retarded readers $U = 178.5$ NS) and the groups did not differ in their memory for order ($U = 150$ NS).


Discussion

(a) Item memory. Both of the predictions derived from the interpretation of Experiment 1 were confirmed by these results. The retarded readers remembered the abstract forms as well as the normal readers; and tracing improved performance equally in both groups. This is strong support for the explanation that differences in memory for the letters reflected differences in the use of phonological memory codes and supports the view that short term visual memory is not a significant cause of reading difficulties. The improvement in memory following tracing amongst normal readers in this experiment is the first demonstration of such an effect in children of normal ability.

The finding of normal visual memory abilities amongst the retarded readers in this study is consistent with much other evidence (reviewed on pp. 25-32). It should be stressed that the requirements of this experiment - memory for a series of forms of similar complexity to letters of the alphabet - are demonstrably similar to those in reading, with the

exception of having no verbal component in this task.  As
such, this experiment and others like it mentioned earlier,
are strong evidence that a deficit in visual memory is not a
common cause of reading retardation.

The problem remains of course that visual problems might
be important for a sub-group of retarded readers.  This
idea has often been advanced and was discussed earlier.
With this in mind the scores of the two groups were compared to determine whether a few retarded readers scored
particularly badly on this task.  No evidence was found to
support this idea.  Looking at the subjects with the lowest
scores revealed that two retarded readers and two normal
readers recognised less than 70 per cent of the forms
across both conditions.  The lowest score in this experiment was actually obtained by a normal reader.  It certainly remains possible that the problems of a few retarded
readers stem from visual memory difficulties;  the present
sample only contained twenty children.  These results do
suggest, however, that if such children exist they are probably quite rare.

(b)  Order memory.  Again no difference was found
between normal and retarded readers in their memory for
order.  In this case there was less reason to expect a difference, previous claims being inconsistent as to whether
any difficulty in order memory was restricted to verbal
stimuli or was also true of abstract stimuli.  Tracing once
again did not improve memory for order and again this may
plausibly be related to the use of discrete forms in the
present experiment.


EXPERIMENT 3.  THE EFFECTS OF TRACING ON
MEMORY FOR LETTER SEQUENCES IN RETARDED AND
NORMAL READERS OF THE SAME READING AGE

Introduction

It is tempting to conclude from the present results that
verbal memory difficulties are a significant cause of reading
retardation.  This conclusion is unwarranted, however,
since as pointed out earlier, differences found between
groups of normal and retarded readers matched for age and
IQ may be the result of the latter group's limited reading
experience rather than a cause of their difficulties.  One
way of reducing this problem of cause and effect is to match

the retarded readers with a group of younger children reading at the same level but whose reading skill is normal for
their age.  If, in this kind of comparison the retarded
readers are still worse on a given task, then the fact that
the two groups have the same reading ability, rules out the
possibility that the retarded readers' poor performance is
merely due to a lack of reading experience.

To see if the differences in memory for letters between
normal and retarded readers found in Experiment 1 tap a
cause of reading difficulties, in the present experiment a
group of younger children matched for reading age and IQ
were seen.  Since no effects of using 3D letters were
observed in Experiment 1, only 2D letters were used here.
Memory was again compared when the letters were looked at
or looked at and traced around.

Two comparisons are of interest here.  First the memory
capacity of the two groups.  Since verbal memory capacity
increases with age (e.g. Harris and Burke, 1972) the differences found between normal and retarded readers in
Experiment 1 may not be found here between groups matched
for reading age but differing in chronological age.

The second comparison of interest is the relative effect
of tracing in the two groups.  The different effects of
tracing in normal and retarded readers in Experiment 1
were interpreted in terms of phonological encoding differences.  There is evidence that the use of such codes increases
with age, at least when pictures of common objects are
memorised (Conrad, 1971).  Consequently, differences in
memory coding, as revealed by differences in the effects of
tracing, may also be absent when groups matched for reading age are compared.


Method

This was essentially identical to that in Experiment 1 except
for there being just two presentation conditions here;  2D-V
and 2D-VT.  Each child again memorised one string of six
letters and two strings of eight letters, the letter strings
being the same as Experiment 1.  Materials were balanced
across presentation conditions as they had been in Experiment 1.  The order of presentation conditions was counterbalanced across subjects.

(a) Subjects.  Nineteen boys and one girl participated in
the experiment.  All of them were reading at or above their

expected age level.    Details of the group together with the
corresponding details of the retarded readers seen in
Experiments 1 and 2 are given in Table 6.    As will be seen
the two groups are very closely matched for reading age and
IQ, but the normal readers are some 2 years 7 months
younger.

TABLE 6  Details of the age, IQ and reading levels of a
group of young normal controls seen in Experiment 3,
compared with the details of the retarded readers seen in
Experiments 1 and 2

|  | Normal readers | Retarded readers | t | p |
|---|---|---|---|---|
| N | 20 | 20 |  |  |
| IQ (WISC) | 107.65 | 108.2 | 0.22 | NS |
| Reading age (Neale) | 8 yr 1 mth | 8 yr 1 mth | 0.01 | NS |
| Chronological age | 7 yr 7 mth | 10 yr 2 mth |  |  |

Results

The results were compared with those of the poor readers in
Experiment 1.    Scoring procedures were identical to those
in Experiment 1.
    (a) Item memory.    The means and standard deviations
for the number of correctly recognised letters for each
group in each condition are shown in Table 7.

TABLE 7  Means and standard deviations for the number of
letters correctly recognised by the young normal readers in
Experiment 3, compared with equivalent figures for the
retarded readers in Experiment 1

|  | V | VT |
|---|---|---|
| Normal readers | 16.80 (2.042) | 17.45 (2.762) |
| Retarded readers | 16.35 (2.254) | 18.45 (1.669) |

(Maximum possible score in each condition is 22.)

The two groups appear to remember a similar number of letters overall, although it is striking that the normal readers remember slightly more than the retarded readers in the V condition, despite being some two and a half years younger. Here again tracing had little effect on memory for letters in the normal readers.

These results were subjected to a 3-way (2 x 2 x 2) analysis of variance with presentation conditions a within subjects factor and order of presentation conditions and reading ability as between subject factors.

Overall more letters were remembered following tracing ($F = 15.2$; d.f. 1, 36; $p < 0.001$). The normal and retarded readers did not differ in their memory for letters ($F < 1$; d.f. 1, 36; NS) but tracing had a differential effect on memory for the letters in the two groups ($F = 4.23$; d.f. 1, 36; $p < 0.05$). This interaction was explored with a Tukey HSD test. Tracing improved memory for letters in the retarded readers ($p < 0.05$) but had no significant effect in the normal readers.

The only other significant effect was the interaction between presentation conditions and their order ($F = 17.49$; d.f. 1, 36; $p < 0.001$). This reflects a decline in performance over trials as occurred in Experiment 2. When the V condition is first, the addition of tracing in the later VT trials does not improve memory while tracing does improve memory when the VT condition is first ($p < 0.01$; Tukey HSD test). Some slight caution is again necessary here since order and stimuli are confounded in the present design. However, two different sets of letter sequences were used in this experiment to make the materials completely comparable with those in Experiment 1. Since the effect holds across these different stimulus materials, and occurs in two different experiments it seems very probably that it is a true order effect and not merely an artefact of the stimuli used.

(b) Order memory. The means and standard deviations for the correlations obtained by the two groups in the two conditions are shown in Table 8.

The two groups seem to remember the order of the letters equally well; if anything the retarded readers being slightly better. It also appears that while tracing aids order memory in the retarded readers, it tends to hinder it in the normal readers. The correlations were subjected to an analysis of variance in the same way as the scores for items correct.

TABLE 8 Means and standard deviations for the values of
tau obtained by the young normal readers in Experiment 3,
compared with equivalent figures for the retarded readers
in Experiment 1

|                  | V             | VT            |
|------------------|---------------|---------------|
| Normal readers   | 0.50 (0.295)  | 0.42 (0.285)  |
| Retarded readers | 0.49 (0.305)  | 0.63 (0.296)  |

The two groups did not differ in their memory for order
($F = 1.58$; d.f. 1, 36; NS) and nor did tracing improve
order memory ($F = 0.38$; d.f. 1, 36; NS). The interaction between reading ability and tracing was significant,
however ($F = 4.5$; d.f. 1, 36; $p < 0.05$); while tracing
tended to improve order memory for the retarded readers
it hindered it slightly for the normal readers. These differences did not reach significance in a Tukey test, however. In view of this, the result should be treated with
caution, especially since in other experiments tracing has
failed to improve order memory. The only other singificant
effect was the interaction between presentation conditions
and their order ($F = 8.31$; d.f. 1, 36; $p < 0.01$). This
reflects the fact that memory for order decreased over
trials, but again comparisons between the means comprising this interaction did not reveal any significant differences. These non-significant a posteriori comparisons
probably reflect the large error variance associated with
tau.

Again, as a further check on the trends revealed by the
analysis of variance, Mann-Whitney U tests were conducted.
These confirmed the findings of the analysis of variance.
The retarded and normal readers did not differ in their
memory for the order of the letters ($U = 155.5$; NS) and
tracing did not reliably improve the retarded readers'
memory for order ($U = 152$; NS).


Discussion

(a) Item memory. The normal readers, although some two
and a half years younger remembered a similar number of
letters to the retarded readers. The retarded readers'
poor memory capacity for letters might, therefore, be
attributed to their limited reading experience. A different

picture emerges from considering the memory codes employed by the two groups. The differential effect of tracing on memory for letters was also present here. This has been explained in terms of a deficiency in phonological memory coding in the retarded readers. If this explanation is accepted, and there is much in its favour, it appears that this characteristic of the retarded readers cannot be attributed to their limited reading experience. At any rate, whatever characteristic of the retarded readers' results in tracing being an effective memory aid for letters, is not simply the result of limited reading experience. It seems likely, therefore, that this characteristic taps a cause of their reading difficulties.

(b) Order memory. The trend for retarded readers to remember the order of letters better than age matched controls in Experiment 1 was absent when comparison was made with younger children matched for reading age. The younger controls were slightly worse than the retarded readers in their memory for order. This confirms the impression given in Experiment 1 that although the retarded readers were worse at remembering the order of the letters than controls this tendency was not particularly marked.

An interesting finding here was the tendency for tracing to aid order memory for the retarded readers and to hinder it for the normal readers. Neither of these trends alone was significant although the interaction of these factors was. Because of this, and the fact that similar trends were not present in Experiment 1, this result should be regarded with considerable caution.


SUMMARY AND CONCLUSIONS

These experiments, together with the other evidence reviewed in Chapter 1, suggest that a major cause of reading retardation is some form of verbal learning difficulty and not any weakness in visual perception and memory. The retarded readers remembered fewer letters than the normal readers, and tracing improved memory for letters only in the retarded readers. In contrast, memory for non-verbal forms was comparable in these two groups and tracing around them had a uniformly beneficial effect on memory. This pattern of results was interpreted in terms of the retarded readers' deficient use of a phonological memory code but normal visual memory abilities. Moreover, the differences between normal and retarded readers in the effects of tracing on memory for letters could not be attributed to the latter groups' limited reading experience. This implies, if the present argument is accepted, that the deficiency in the use of phonological memory coding amongst retarded readers cannot simply be a consequence of their limited reading ability or experience. This makes it somewhat more likely that this difficulty relates to the source of these children's reading problems.

The evidence for deficient speech coding in memory by retarded readers was discussed earlier (pp. 49-51). There are some clear and specific similarities between the findings in Experiment 1 and those of Spring and Capps (1974) which were described then. Both experiments show the poor short term verbal memory abilities of retarded readers. The unsystematic observations in Experiment 1 which suggested the retarded readers relied less on verbal rehearsal are supported by Spring and Capps systematic observations of the scanning strategies of these children while performing a probed digit recall task.

Another factor of interest in the present experiments is the effects of tracing. The selective improvement amongst the retarded readers in their memory for letters following tracing suggests that teaching methods incorporating such a motor element may be of special help to these children when learning to read. Experiment 1 is consistent with others (pp. 62-5) in showing that tracing selectively improves memory for visually presented verbal materials in retarded readers. Experiment 2 extended this by showing that for non-verbal forms tracing has an equally beneficial effect on memory in normal and retarded readers. This finding also gives us a plausible explanation for the selective improvement in memory for verbal materials following tracing in retarded readers. While the normal children recode such material into a speech-like form, the retarded readers appear unable or reluctant to do so, and appear to rely more on an alternative visual memory code. The tracing appears to improve such visual memory processes.

This explanation of the effects of tracing on memory for verbal materials in retarded readers, also has the advantage of being consistent with evidence about their cognitive abilities. This improvement in memory for verbal materials following tracing is seen to depend upon their poor verbal memory skills for which there is much independent evidence, and more specifically on their reluctance to use a phonological memory code (pp. 49-51).

However, this explanation also raises a paradox. It appears that most retarded readers do not suffer any weakness of visual memory (pp. 29-32). On the contrary it seems likely that tracing improves their memory for letters, precisely because they rely on a strategy of remembering them as visual configurations rather than in terms of their names. This leaves the problem of how tracing might help them learn to read. According to evidence reviewed in Chapter 1, their problem in learning to read is unlikely to be one of remembering the visual configuration of words, but rather one of learning the verbal labels of these visual configurations. It is not immediatley clear how a procedure which improves visual recognition could improve verbal associative learning of this sort. This problem will be returned to later.

It is also interesting to consider in relation to this argument, the possibility that a sub-group of retarded readers experience visual memory problems. Since tracing has been shown in these experiments to improve visual recognition, remedial teaching which incorporates tracing might reasonably be expected to help such children.

Another question raised by these experiments is the effect of tracing on memory for order. Learning to read clearly involves learning to recognise the sequences of letters which compose words; the order of the letters as well as the letters themselves must be remembered. In the present experiments, however, tracing has only been shown to improve memory for individual items and not for their order. This raises the question fo whether tracing is capable of improving memory for order, since although such effects are absent in the present experiments they presumably might be important in learning to read. One possible explanation for these negative results in the present experiments derives from the use of discrete forms. Tracing in remedial teaching is used in conjunction with words written in cursive script. The absence of any effect of tracing on order memory in the present experiments might derive from the use of discrete letters and forms. This issue will be explored in some subsequent experiments during this book.

Finally, perhaps the major theoretical question raised by these experiments concerns the mechanisms responsible for the improvement in memory following tracing. Two broad types of explanation suggest themselves here. First, one might argue that tracing serves to direct attention to the material to be memorised. An alternative might be in terms

of the information in memory about the tracing movements.
This could provide an additional source of information which
improves visual recognition.   It is to this theoretical
question that the next experiments are addressed.

# 4 The mechanisms underlying the enhancement of visual recognition following tracing

## INTRODUCTION

Previous experiments have demonstrated that in a serial memory task tracing around abstract shapes or letters whilst simultaneously looking at them, results in better performance than does simply looking at them. The present chapter examines the mechanism responsible for this effect. Two types of explanation suggest themselves. According to the first, tracing simply concentrates attention during presentation of the items. An alternative attributes the effects of tracing to the operation of a separate motor memory system. In this view two equivalent sources of information are available after tracing; these are visual memory for the shapes and memory for the movements made whilst tracing around them. The addition of movement information then aids visual recognition.

These two types of explanation are not of course mutually exclusive. The attentional hypothesis is vague and difficult to test. There is no direct measure of whether or not a subject is attending to material which he is asked to memorise. In the previous experiments a finger pointing response was used to control for such attentional effects. This is obviously less than perfect. Although in order to point to stimuli the subject must at least look at them, more subtle differences between conditions are left uncontrolled.

There are, however, some arguments which reduce the plausibility of an explanation of the effects of tracing cast solely in attentional terms. The presentation of the letters and shapes in Experiments 1, 2 and 3 was unhurried and subjects generally appeared well motivated to succeed at the task which was novel, and apparently enjoyable to them. In these circumstances it is hard to see how a simple attention attracting procedure could improve performance.

Another argument concerns the differential effects of tracing on memory for verbal materials in normal and retarded readers. Without additional assumptions it is not clear how this effect can be explained in attentional terms. The equivalent effects of tracing on memory in the two groups when nonsense forms were used shows that the retarded readers did not suffer from a general attentional deficit.

A final argument against the primacy of attention as an explanation of tracing's effects comes from considering studies of the effects of haptic inspection on the subsequent visual recognition of abstract forms. These experiments have uniformly failed to provide evidence for improvements in memory following the addition of haptic inspection. Millar (1971) with children, and Cashdan and Zung (1970) and Zung, Butter and Cashdan (1974) with adult subjects, found that visually inspected forms were remembered no differently to those visually and haptically inspected while Fico and Brodsky (1972) actually found memory performance to be significantly worse in the latter of these two conditions. With 3- to 4-year-old children a paradigm involving memory for a single shape over a long period (2 days) has yielded conflicting results. Denner and Cashdan (1967) found that visual recognition of a two-dimensional shape (hexagon) was superior when the shape was handled directly or while encased in a clear plastic sphere, compared to a control condition when the un-encased shape was inspected visually. Weiner and Goodnow (1970) showed that this effect was an attentional one. They compared recognition in a visual and visual plus handling condition when all objects were encased in a clear plastic sphere, and found identical levels of performance. Thus for three-dimensional objects, which these young children find more interesting than two-dimensional ones, handling has no effect on memory. In summary, additional haptic exploration of visual stimuli which are to be remembered for short periods does not have any beneficial effect on memory in children or adults. With longer retention periods with young children as subjects handling may improve memory due to its attention directing properties but only for objects the children do not find particularly interesting.

Since tracing is effective in aiding visual recognition, while haptic inspection fails to do so, a purely attentional explanation of the effects of tracing seem untenable. There is no reason to suppose that haptic inspection of a form should have less attention directing value than tracing around the outline of a form.

Although such arguments may reduce the plausibility of a purely attentional explanation of the effects of tracing, they are clearly not conclusive.  The experiments in this chapter aim to obtain direct evidence for or against the operation of separate visual and motor memory traces in the recognition of forms following tracing.  For this purpose an interference procedure was adopted to try and produce selective impairments in performance.  Since such procedures are relatively complex, it was felt that they may be more appropriate for use with adult subjects than with children.  If this was to be done, however, it was first necessary to demonstrate that tracing could have a beneficial effect on visual recognition in adults, as it had in children.  It was in order to provide such a demonstration that the next experiment was conducted.


EXPERIMENT 4.  THE EFFECT OF TRACING UPON
MEMORY FOR SERIES OF GRAPHIC FORMS:
A REPLICATION WITH ADULT SUBJECTS

Introduction

The aim of this experiment was simply to investigate whether the beneficial effect of tracing on the visual recognition of forms found in children was also true of adult subjects.  Theoretically, there seemed no reason to suppose that such an effect which was present in children of normal ability should not also be found with adults.  A demonstration that this was the case would enable subsequent experiments with adults to explore the mechanisms responsible for this effect.  Such a demonstration would also be of interest in showing that the effect of tracing on visual memory had some generality.


Method

(a) Subjects.  Twenty adults, eleven women and nine men, drawn from the Oxford subject panel, participated in this experiment.  They were paid for their participation.
  (b) Design.  A short term memory task was used which

was very similar to that in Experiment 2. The same set of fourteen abstract forms were used as stimuli. Once again, there were two conditions; visual (V), and visual plus tracing (VT), and all subjects participated in both conditions. Within each condition there were four trials; on the first two of these, seven forms were presented to be remembered, while on each of the last two trials, eight shapes were presented. The stimuli were counterbalanced across conditions. The order of presentation conditions was counterbalanced across subjects, half the subjects had the V condition first, and half had this condition second.

(c) Procedure. Subjects were tested individually in a quiet room. Testing was completed in one session lasting approximately 45 minutes.

In a pilot study it was found that some adults tended to employ a verbal strategy to remember the shapes. It was felt that this would complicate the results, since it had been hypothesised earlier that tracing only improved the recognition of forms remembered in visual, and not in phonological terms. In order to avoid these possible complications due to the use of verbal coding, subjects were required to count backwards in threes throughout the stimulus presentation and delay periods. This also served to make the task more difficult and so avoid likely ceiling effects, in an otherwise fairly simple task for adult subjects. Subjects were given typewritten instructions to read as follows:

This experiment is concerned with memory for shapes. At the beginning of each trial I will say a three-figure number; when you hear this, repeat it and count backwards from it, in 3s, out loud. Following this I will uncover a series of 7 or 8 shapes which you are to try and remember in order.

When you have inspected the shapes, I will cover and remove them. Please continue to count. After a short delay you will be shown an array of 14 shapes which contains the shapes which you saw. You should then stop counting and reconstruct the series you saw, guessing if you are uncertain about any of the shapes or the order in which they occurred.

For the first four trials you will look at the shapes, whilst in the second set of four trials you will look at the shapes and simultaneously trace around each shape with your index finger. OR (For the first four trials you will look at the shapes and simultaneously trace around each shape with your index finger. For the second set of four trials you will just look at the shapes.)

When tracing, use the index finger of the hand with which you write.  Make a slow definite movement, with your finger touching the surface of the card, mimicking the act of drawing the shape.  Trace each shape just once in order from left to right.  When you have completed this, carry on looking at the shapes until they are covered up.

Before the experiment began the subjects were asked if they had any questions.  The experimenter then paraphrased the instructions to ensure comprehension and stressed that subjects should count backwards in threes as quickly and as evenly as possible throughout the experiment.

On both the V and VT trials the series of forms was presented for 45 seconds.  This had been shown to be long enough for the subject to trace around each form without hurrying, and indeed was longer than subjects generally required.  They were timed with a stop-watch.  In order to enable presentation time to be controlled the stimuli were presented using pairs of card sheets.  Before each trial the experimenter arranged the series of shapes on one card, out of sight of the subject, and then covered it with an identical card.  This was then placed on the table in front of the subject.  When the subject was ready the experimenter uncovered the array of shapes and simultaneously started the stop-watch.  After 45 seconds, the experimenter placed the cover over the series and removed them from in front of the subject.  A delay of 1 minute 15 seconds followed.  During this time the experimenter mixed the cards presented to be memorised with the remaining cards by shuffling them.  The mixed set of fourteen was then laid out in two rows of seven between two larger card sheets.  This arrangement was then placed on the table in front of the subject and at the end of the delay period the experimenter removed the cover exposing the set of fourteen cards to the subject.  The subject then took as long as desired to pick out the seven or eight cards remembered and arrange them in order.

Results

The scoring of results was identical to previous experiments.

(a)  Item memory.  In each condition the maximum possible score was 30 (two trials with seven and two trials with eight forms to remember). The means and standard deviations of these scores are presented in Table 9.

TABLE 9  The means and standard deviations for the number of forms correctly recognised in each condition of Experiment 4

| Presentation condition | |
|---|---|
| Visual | Visual and tracing |
| 23.30 | 25.00 |
| (2.577) | (2.753) |

(The maximum possible score in each condition is 30.)

It appears clear from these results that the adults, like the children in Experiment 2, recognise more forms correctly when they have traced them.

The scores for the number of correctly recognised forms were subjected to a two-way (2 x 2) analysis of variance with presentation conditions a within subject variable and order of presentation conditions a between subjects variable. Only the main effect of presentation conditions reached significance ($F = 17.938$; d.f. 1, 18; $p < 0.001$) which showed that items were remembered better following tracing.

(b) Order memory. Kendall's tau was calculated for each trial and the value for the four trials within each condition were then averaged. The means and standard deviations of these scores are presented in Table 10.

TABLE 10  The means and standard deviations for the values of tau in the two conditions of Experiment 4

| Presentation condition | |
|---|---|
| Visual | Visual and tracing |
| 0.42 | 0.50 |
| (0.346) | (0.203) |

These correlations were subjected to an analysis of variance in the same way as the scores for items correct. No effects reached an acceptable level of significance. There was a weak trend for order to be remembered better following tracing ($F = 1.579$; d.f. 1, 18; NS) and a trend towards

an interaction between presentation conditions and their
order (F = 2.11, d.f. 1, 18;  NS).

## Discussion

These findings are consistent with those of earlier studies
in which children were the subjects.   The beneficial effects
of tracing on item memory clearly have some generality.
Conversely, tracing does not appear to have any reliable
effects on memory for the order of items in this situation.
Given this demonstration that tracing can improve the visual
recognition of forms in adults as well as in children, the
next experiment, also with adults, aimed to explore the
mechanisms responsible for this effect.

## EXPERIMENT 5.   THE EFFECTS OF MOTOR INTERFER-ENCE ON MEMORY FOR GRAPHIC FORMS FOLLOWING TRACING

### Introduction

The aim of the present experiment is to test a simple
theoretical account of how tracing may improve the visual
recognition of two-dimensional forms.   According to this
account, when the subject has looked at and traced a form,
there exist in memory two distinct representations of that
form.   There is a visual representation of the form, and
there is also a representation coded in terms of the movements performed while tracing it.   For the sake of brevity
these two representations will be referred to as visual and
motor memory traces.

The use of the term motor memory perhaps needs some
brief justification here.   The term kinaesthetic was used by
Fernald and others to refer to the teaching methods which
prompted these experiments.   This conveys a sense of
passivity, since kinaesthetic is often used to refer to the
sensations produced by muscle and joint receptors during
movements.   The term motor memory will be used here to
stress that following tracing both efferent and afferent
information is potentially available in memory, i.e., information about the motor commands that produced the tracing
movement and feedback from muscle and joint receptors
about the movement produced.   The use of the term motor

leaves open the question of the extent to which each of these theoretically separable forms of information are encoded in memory.

The next problem is how such a motor memory trace, resulting from tracing movements, could improve visual recognition. The first point to note here, is that tracing could theoretically give rise to enough information about a form to be useful. Tracing demands that the subject perform a movement which completely defines the two-dimensional line form under inspection. If such a movement were remembered it would embody all the information necessary to specify such a form at a later time.

Given that such movement information is remembered, how could it improve visual recognition? For this to occur it is necessary to postulate some integration of the visual and motor information in memory. Such an idea is certainly not unreasonable, however. It seems necessary for a variety of reasons to postulate a mechanism for translation between visual and motor information. Such a mechanism would, for example, presumably be necessary for performing visually guided movements.

In order to test this account an interference procedure was adopted, which was designed to selectively interfere with the motor memory trace produced by tracing. Short term memory for abstract forms was again tested either with or without tracing them. A motor interference task was then introduced on some trials in each presentation condition. It was predicted that if following tracing a distinct motor memory trace existed which aided performance, there would be a differential effect of the interference task in the two conditions, i.e., the interference task ought to be more disruptive when it follows the occurrence of tracing in the presentation condition. This assumes the susceptibility of any putative motor memory system to interference from subsequent movements. At least in the rather different situation of lever positioning tasks there is ample evidence that motor memory is susceptible to such interference (Faust-Adams, 1972; Kantowitz, 1972; Williams, Beaver, Spence and Rundell, 1969).


Method

Except for the differences described below the method employed was the same as Experiment 4.

(a) Subjects. Twenty-eight adults, twenty-one women
and seven men, recruited from the Oxford subject panel,
were paid to participate in the experiment.

(b) Design. A short term memory task was used in
which subjects attempted to remember a series of seven
forms on each of eight trials. The experiment was split
into two blocks of four trials. In one block the subject
looked at the forms (V condition) and in the other simultaneously traced around them (VT condition). Within each
block of four trials the middle two trials were the interference trials. Order of presentation conditions was counterbalanced across subjects. Half the subjects performed the
V condition first and half had this condition second.
Stimuli were counterbalanced across conditions, and within
each condition stimuli were counterbalanced across interference and non-interference trials.

(c) Procedure. The basic format of each trial was identical to Experiment 4, with the exception that the delay
period was in this case 1 minute 30 seconds instead of
1 minute 15 seconds.

Before the experiment began, the subjects were given the
same instructions to read as those used in Experiment 4.
In addition, immediately before the first interference trial
subjects were given the following instructions to read:

During the next two trials I would like you to perform an
additional task during the delay between memorising the
series of shapes, and reconstructing it. This consists
of feeling a series of four shapes which cannot be seen as
they are covered by a cloth. The shapes are formed by
cutting grooves in the cards, and consist of the same
shapes as used throughout this experiment. You should
identify each of the four shapes by running your index
finger around the groove on each card. Make sure you
get a clear impression of which shape is represented on
each card. When you have completed this you should say
whether any two of the four shapes you felt were the
same, or whether they were all different.

The interference trials were therefore identical to the
non-interference trials, except for the addition of the motor
interference task during the delay period. The stimuli used
for the interference task were tactually distinct enlarged
(x 2) versions of the same stimuli used in the memory task.
They were formed by cutting grooves 0.6 cm wide in cards
which were then backed by another thickness of card.
These were mounted in rows of four with even spaces

between each card. Four sets were constructed; in two
cases the first and last cards bore identical shapes while in
the other two cases all the cards bore different shapes.

The interference stimuli were placed on the table in
front of the subject immediately after the memory series had
been removed, and were covered by a brown cloth to prevent
the subject seeing them. Subjects felt the stimuli by placing
their hand under the cloth. Instructing the subjects to run
their fingers around the pattern formed by the grooves meant
that they performed highly similar movements to those performed in the VT condition. This interference task was
demonstrated immediately before the first interference trial,
with a set of four interference stimuli not used in the experiment. Within each condition, comprising four trials, the
middle two were always interference trials, and of these
two, one trial always presented a set of interfering stimuli
containing two stimuli which were identical.

The relationship between interference stimuli and memory
stimuli was considered to be of possible importance, since
it was not known whether any possible effects of interference
would depend upon the similarity of the two sets of forms or
the motor activity per se. Within each pair of interference
trials, on one trial the four interference stimuli contained
two forms which were also in the set of memory stimuli, and
on the other, there was just one such form in common. The
data were examined for any effects of the degree of similarity between memory and interference stimuli, but no
trends were present.


Results

The scoring of results was identical to that in previous
experiments.

(a) Item memory. The means and standard deviations for
the number of forms correctly recognised (out of fourteen)
for each of the four conditions are presented in Table 11.

There are several trends in these data which are note-
worthy. As in previous experiments, in the absence of any
interference more forms are recognised in the VT condition
than in the V condition. The motor interference task does
appear to impair performance, and more interestingly, as
predicted, it appears to be most disruptive in the VT condition.

The results were subjected to a 3-way (2 x 2 x 2) analysis

TABLE 11 Means and standard deviations for the number of forms correctly recognised in each condition of Experiment 5

|  |  | Motor interference | |
|  |  | Absent | Present |
| --- | --- | --- | --- |
| Presentation | Visual | 11.43 (1.834) | 11.29 (2.106) |
| Condition | Visual and tracing | 12.04 (1.261) | 10.96 (1.856) |

(The maximum possible score in each condition is 14.)

of variance with presentation conditions (V or VT) and interference as within subject variables and order of presentation conditions as a between subjects variable.

The only significant effect in this analysis was that of interference ($F = 4.76$; d.f. 1, 26; $p < 0.05$) indicating that performance was significantly worse on interference than non-interference trials. The trend noted above for interference to be most disruptive in the VT condition failed to reach an acceptable level of significance ($F = 3.49$; d.f. 1, 26; $p < 0.10$). Because this interaction failed to reach significance no a posteriori tests were applied. It is clear, however, from inspecting the means, that as in previous experiments, in the absence of interference the forms tend to be recognised better following tracing.

(b) Order memory. Tau was again calculated for each trial and a score for each subject in each condition obtained by averaging the value for the two trials. The means and standard deviations of these values of tau are shown in Table 12.

TABLE 12 The means and standard deviations for the values of tau in each condition of Experiment 5

|  |  | Motor interference | |
|  |  | Absent | Present |
| --- | --- | --- | --- |
| Presentation | Visual | 0.52 (0.332) | 0.50 (0.283) |
| Condition | Visual and tracing | 0.54 (0.230) | 0.49 (0.254) |

It is clear that these values are very similar to each other.  This was confirmed by a 3-way (2 x 2 x 2) analysis of variance of these scores, with presentation conditions and presence or absence of interference as within subject variables, and order of conditions a between subjects variable.  As expected from inspecting the means in Table 12, no effects in this analysis approached significance.

Discussion

The prediction of the hypothesis which prompted this experiment was that there would be an interaction between presentation conditions and the presence or absence of the motor interference task.  If the improvement in visual recognition performance following tracing depends on the existence of a distinct motor memory trace, then a procedure which selectively interferes with this trace ought to be most disruptive to performance in the VT condition.  Although this pattern of results failed to reach statistical significance, there were clear trends in the data in this direction.

Two factors in the present experiment may have served to reduce the expected interaction between presentation conditions and interference.  First, performance was at a very high level for some subjects.  Because of this the effects of interference may have been reduced by the occurrence of perfect or near perfect performance on some trials.  A second factor relates to the counting procedure.  Subjects varied in their ability to count backwards in threes, and more importantly the same subject often varied his counting rate across trials, some subjects requiring frequent prompting from the experimenter to maintain an adequate rate.  For example, subjects occasionally commented after a trial that they had concentrated more on the counting procedure than on other trials, and offered this as an excuse for what they considered (often accurately) to have been poor memory performance on that trial.  The size of such effects is hard to estimate.  It is clear, however, that the counting procedure inevitably introduced noise into the data with a concomitant increase in the error variance and a reduction of the statistical significance of any systematic trends present.

There is little to say about the results on order memory here.  As in previous experiments, tracing failed to improve order memory.  Also, there was no trend towards an interaction between presentation conditions and interference in these data. Both these results are consistent with the view that in the present experimental situation tracing acts on the retention of item and not order information.

In conclusion, although the main prediction of this experiment was not confirmed, there were certainly strong trends in the data in the predicted direction. Because of this, and the factors noted above which appeared likely to reduce the predicted effect, it was decided to explore the issue further. A reasonable way to do this appeared to be to replicate the experiment using children as subjects. This would remove the two factors tentatively identified as causes for the non-significance of the interaction between presentation conditions and interference. First, the children's performance would be likely to be lower than that of adults removing the complication of ceiling effects. Second, there would be no need to have a counting distractor task because it appeared from previous experiments that children of the ages studied did not try to remember the forms in verbal terms. Familiarity with the procedure of this experiment suggested that it would not be too complicated for use with 8- to 9-year-old children, if care were taken in explaining it.

EXPERIMENT 6. THE EFFECTS OF MOTOR INTERFERENCE ON MEMORY FOR GRAPHIC FORMS FOLLOWING TRACING: A REPLICATION WITH CHILDREN

Method

The method of this experiment was essentially identical to that in Experiment 5 except for two points. All instructions were given verbally by the experimenter and there was no counting distractor task.

The children were tested individually in a quiet room in their school, each session lasting approximately 50 minutes. During the session the experimenter and the subject sat side by side in front of a pair of tables. A screen enabled the experimenter to manipulate stimuli and to record responses out of the subject's sight. No knowledge of results was given but the experimenter encouraged the subjects to maintain their interest and motivation.

The experiment was presented as a 'remembering game' involving shapes. Presentation of test trials was preceded by a demonstration trial in which a series of three shapes was presented for the subject to remember. This was not scored and served to familiarise subjects with the procedure used throughout the experiment. When the VT condition was first, the subjects traced around the demonstration series of three shapes and this was the only demonstration they received. For subjects who had the V condition first, the act of tracing was demonstrated and practised by them immediately before the VT trials, using the same series of three shapes. Similarly, before the first interference trial the interference task was demonstrated to the subject and it was explained that this would be an additional task to perform instead of 'just waiting' between memorising the set of stimuli and reconstructing it.

(a) Subjects. Twenty-four children, 13 boys and 11 girls whose mean age was 8 years 7 months (ranging from 8.0 years to 9 years 2 months), served as subjects. They were seen at three schools in the Oxford area.

Results

The scoring of results was identical to previous experiments.

(a) Item memory. In each condition the maximum possible score was 14 (two trials in each with seven shapes presented). The means and standard deviations for these scores are presented in Table 13. The same results are illustrated graphically in Figure 1.

TABLE 13 Means and standard deviations for the number of forms correctly recognised in each condition of Experiment 6

|  |  | Motor interference | |
|  |  | Absent | Present |
| --- | --- | --- | --- |
| Presentation | Visual | 11.417 (1.100) | 10.875 (1.676) |
| Condition | Visual and tracing | 12.375 (1.172) | 10.75 (2.005) |

(The maximum possible score in each condition is 14.)

These data are similar to those obtained in Experiment 5. Once again in the absence of interference more forms are correctly recognised in the VT condition. More interestingly, the effects of interference again seem more marked in the VT condition.

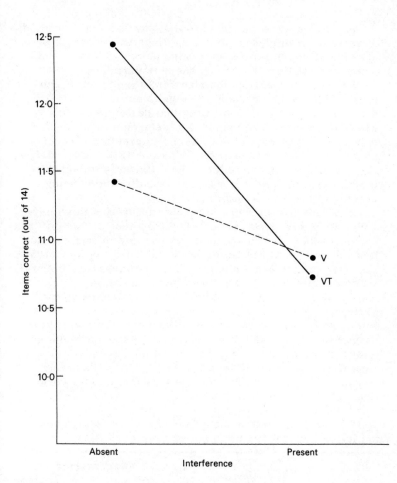

FIGURE 1  Mean number of items correct as a function of presentation conditions and presence or absence of inter- ference in Experiment 6

The scores were subjected to a 3-way (2 x 2 x 2) analysis of variance with presentation conditions and presence or absence of interference, as within subject variables and order of conditions a between subjects variable.

The analysis confirms the above interpretation.  The main effect of interference was significant (F = 16.767; d.f. 1, 22;  p < 0.001) indicating that performance was worse on interference than non-interference trials.  The only other significant effect was the interaction between interference and presentation conditions (F = 7.109;  d.f. 1, 22;  p < 0.025).  This reflects the differential effect of interference in the two conditions, the disruption being greater in the VT condition.

The means for the four conditions comprising this inter-action were examined by the Tukey HSD test.  Two differences reached significance;  in the absence of interference items are remembered better in the VT condition (p < 0.05), and interference had a significant effect on memory in the VT condition (p < 0.01) but not in the V condition.

(b)  Order memory.  Kendall's tau was calculated for performance on each trial and the value for the two trials within each condition were then averaged.  In a very few cases when less than three items were recognised on a given trial a correlation was not calculated and the value for that condition was based on the other trial only.  The means and standard deviations of the correlations for the four conditions are shown in Table 14.

TABLE 14  Means and standard deviations for the values of tau in the four conditions in Experiment 6

|  |  | Motor interference | |
|  |  | Absent | Present |
| --- | --- | --- | --- |
| Presentation | Visual | 0.43 (0.349) | 0.31 (0.378) |
| Condition | Visual and tracing | 0.41 (0.371) | 0.25 (0.486) |

This pattern of results is clearly quite different to that for items correct.  Tracing does not appear to improve memory for the order of items as it did for the items themselves. Furthermore, there is no sign of any differential effect of interference in the different conditions, though interference does impair memory for the order of items overall.

The correlations were subjected to an analysis of variance with presentation conditions and presence or absence of interference as within subject variables and order of conditions as between subjects variable.

The main effect of interference was again significant ($F = 7.16$; d.f. 1, 22; $p < 0.05$) demonstrating that interference disturbs memory for order independently of any effect it may have on item memory. The interaction between presentation conditions and interference was in this case insignificant ($F = 0.227$; d.f. 1, 22; NS). This together with the absence of any significant main effect of presentation conditions, indicates that tracing, in this experimental situation does not improve memory for the order of items although it was shown previously to improve memory for the items themselves. The only other significant term in the analysis was the 3-way interaction between interference, presentation conditions, and order of presentation conditions ($F = 22.04$; d.f. 1, 22; $p < 0.001$).

This is illustrated graphically in Figure 2. Within the first block, interference is highly disruptive to memory for order, whilst in the second block it is less so. However, the degree of disruption in the first block depends upon the

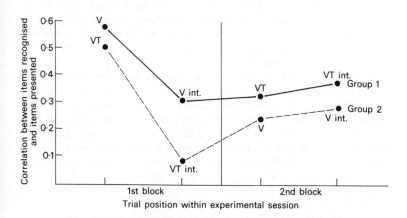

FIGURE 2 Correlation between the order of correctly recognised items and their order of presentation as a function of experimental conditions and their position within the experimental session in Experiment 6

presentation mode and is most marked when tracing has occurred at presentation. This result is difficult to explain, but presumably relates to the adoption of strategies by the subject to overcome the disruptive effects of interference, and to the fact that, before such strategies emerge, retention of order is most impaired after the occurrence of tracing. In this design, however, stimuli are confounded with order, and the effects of these two variables cannot therefore be separated.

This complex pattern of results finds no counterpart in the previous experiment. Such a difference is hard to explain. It may reflect the age difference in the subjects of the two experiments or it could be due to the use of the backward counting distractor task in Experiment 5.


Discussion

The findings of this experiment are consistent with those of previous experiments in showing that tracing improves the visual recognition of abstract graphic forms. In addition these findings support the idea that this improvement reflects the operation of a distinct motor memory system. There are differential effects of the motor interference task on memory for forms that have been traced around compared to those just visually inspected, and these effects clearly indicate some differential encoding of the items. The form of these effects is compatible with the operation of a distinct motor memory system.

It is notable that in the present experiment the interaction between presentation conditions and interference was significant, while this interaction failed to reach significance in the previous experiment, where adults were the subjects. Obviously we cannot be sure about the causes of this difference between experiments. These findings do at least increase the plausibility of the idea that the counting procedure used in the previous experiment added noise to the data which tended to reduce the significance of the trend towards this interaction.

No particular predictions were made concerning the effects of tracing or interference on memory for the order of the items. Since tracing without interference failed to produce any beneficial effects on memory for the order of items, it is not surprising that the motor interference task did not have differential effects on memory for the order of items in the two presentation conditions. These findings support the view that in this situation tracing aids item memory and not order memory.

The complex 3-way interaction between the effects of interference, presentation conditions, and their order was quite unexpected, and implies that order memory is sensitive to the effects of trial position within a session. This remains a tentative conclusion, however, since in the present experiment stimuli are confounded with order.

## EXPERIMENT 7. THE EFFECTS OF VISUAL INTERFERENCE ON MEMORY FOR GRAPHIC FORMS FOLLOWING TRACING

### Introduction

Experiment 6 demonstrated that tracing around forms improved memory for them and that a motor interference task had a differential effect on memory for forms, depending upon whether they were traced around during the presentation period. This was interpreted as supporting the view that the beneficial effect of tracing on memory represents the effect of a separate motor memory system. This effect, however, has not been shown to be specifically related to the motor interference task. One might argue, for example, that the higher level of performance displayed following tracing is generally more susceptible to any form of interference between presentation and recognition testing. Alternatively, it might be argued that the decrement on interference trials in this experiment was an artefact which arose because the interference task always occurred on the middle two trials of each block. Such a decrement in performance on the middle trials might conceivably occur in the absence of any interfering task, perhaps because of the build up of proactive interference. If this argument were accepted the differential effect of interference in the different presentation conditions would presumably have to be explained in terms of possible regression effects mentioned earlier, i.e., in terms of the higher level of performance in the VT condition being generally more susceptible to disruption. The present ecperiment aimed to explore these possible objections by examining the effects of a visual interference task in the same situation.

It was expected that the effects of visual interference on

memory in the V and VT conditions would be less clear-cut than the effects of motor interference, since performance in both conditions is presumed to depend primarily on visual memory.  If a visual interference task selectively impairs visual memory we would expect a roughly equal decrease in the number of items correct in both conditions.  This leads to the prediction of a weak interaction between presentation conditions and interference;  performance in the VT condition being slightly less impaired than performance in the V condition, due to a small but unimpaired motor memory component.

Such a pattern of results would rule out the possibility that the effects of interference in Experiment 1 were due to non-specific factors such as trial position.  If visual and motor interference have different effects on performance depending on the presentation condition, then any explanation in terms of such non-specific effects is clearly inadequate.


Method

The method employed was identical to that used in Experiment 6, except for the substitution of an equivalent visual interference task for the motor interference task.
Stimuli for the visual interference task were identical to the stimuli used throughout these experiments.  The actual sets of four forms used were the same as those in the motor interference task.

The visual interference task also required the subjects to judge whether the set of four stimuli presented were all different or whether any two were the same as each other. In order to make the visual task of reasonable difficulty and truly comparable to the motor task the visual stimuli were presented sequentially by placing them on the table in front of the subject, one on top of the other.  They were presented after 45 seconds of the 1 minute 30 second delay period had elapsed, and each card was shown to the subject for 5 seconds.  The slow sequential presentation of the visual stimuli made the task comparable to the motor task and the memory load imposed resulted in significant interference with recognition of the originally memorised sequence of shapes.

(a) Subjects.  A further 24 children drawn from two schools in the Oxford area served as subjects.  There were

12 boys and 12 girls, whose mean age was 8 years 11 months with a range from 8 years 6 months, to 9 years 6 months.

## Results

The scoring of results was identical to that in previous experiments.

(a) Item memory.  The means and standard deviations for the number of forms correctly recognised in each of the four conditions are given in Table 15.   These results are illustrated graphically in Figure 3.

TABLE 15  Means and standard deviations for the number of items correct in each of the four conditions of Experiment 7

|  |  | Motor interference | |
|  |  | Absent | Present |
|---|---|---|---|
| Presentation | Visual | 11.38 (1.279) | 10.54 (1.615) |
| Condition | Visual and tracing | 12.25 (1.188) | 11.83 (1.403) |

(The maximum possible score in each condition is 14.)

This pattern of results is similar to that in Experiment 1, except for the effects of interference in the two presentation conditions.   Items are again remembered better following tracing and the visual interference task reduces memory for items in both conditions.   There is a trend, however, as predicted, for this interference effect to operate in the opposite direction to that obtained with the motor interference task, i.e., visual interference is relatively more disruptive in the visual presentation condition.

The scores for items correct were subjected to a 3-way (2 x 2 x 2) analysis of variance with presentation conditions and presence or absence of interference as within subject variables and order of conditions a   between subjects variable.

In this analysis two main effects were significant, interference produced a decrement in memory ($F = 8.10$; d.f. 1, 22; $p < 0.01$) and tracing improved memory ($F = 21.15$; d.f. 1, 22;   $p < 0.001$).

The trend for the effects of visual interference to be

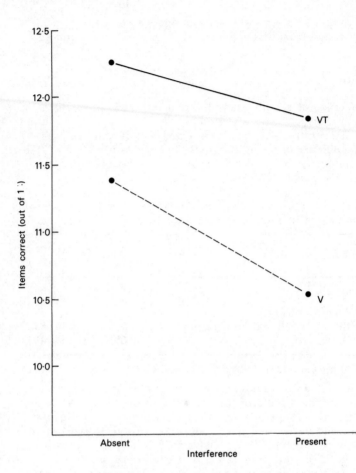

FIGURE 3 Mean number of items correct as a function of presentation conditions and presence or absence of interference in Experiment 7

greater following visual presentation did not lead to a
significant interaction between interference and presentation conditions ($F = 0.055$; d.f. 1, 22; NS), and nor was
a stronger trend towards a 3-way interaction between
interference, presentation conditions, and their order
($F = 3.18$; d.f. 1, 22; NS).   The latter reflects the fact
that within the first block of four trials, interference is
far more disruptive in the V condition, but in the second
block of four trials interference is slightly more disruptive
in the VT condition.   This trend is also uninterpretable due
to the confounding of stimuli and order of presentation conditions.

(i)   Comparison of Experiments 6 and 7.   In order to
explore further the differences between these two experiments in the pattern of results for items correct, the data
for both were combined into a single 4-way (2 x 2 x 2 x 2)
analysis of variance.   Here presence or absence of interference and presentation conditions (V or VT) were within
subject factors and order of presentation conditions and
type of interference (motor interference in Experiment 6,
and visual interference in Experiment 7) were between subjects factors.   The results of this analysis confirmed what
has been said previously.

The main effects of interference ($F = 24.69$; d.f. 1, 44;
$p < 0.001$) and presentation conditions ($F = 18.21$; d.f. 1,
44; $p < 0.001$) were significant, indicating that across both
experiments interference produced a decrement in performance and tracing produced an improvement.   Two interactions also reached significance.   The interaction
between interference, presentation conditions, and type of
interference was significant ($F = 4.70$; d.f. 1, 44;
$p < 0.05$).   This confirms what has been said before;   the
motor (Experiment 6) and visual (Experiment 7) interference
tasks have different effects depending on presentation conditions.   The difference between the effects of visual and
motor interference in the two presentation conditions is
particularly important.   The fact that motor interference is
most disruptive in the VT condition, while visual interference is most disruptive in the V condition, shows that these
interference effects are truly modality specific.   Any
explanation in more general terms such as a decrement in
performance over trials would not cover this pattern of
results across the two experiments.

The interaction between interference, order of presentation conditions and type of interference was also significant

($F = 4.24$; d.f. 1, 33; $p < 0.05$).   This reflects the fact
that in Experiment 1 interference was most disruptive when
the VT condition was first, while in Experiment 2 interference was most disruptive when the V condition was first,
but again the effects of order are confounded with stimulus
effects.

(b) Order memory.   Kendall's tau was again calculated
for each trial.   The means and standard deviations of these
correlations for the four conditions are shown in Table 16.

TABLE 16 Means and standard deviations of the correlations
between the order of correctly recognised items and their
order of presentation in the four conditions in Experiment 7

|  |  | Visual interference | |
|  |  | Absent | Present |
| --- | --- | --- | --- |
| Presentation | Visual | 0.42 (0.406) | 0.36 (0.354) |
| Condition | Visual and tracing | 0.45 (0.380) | 0.39 (0.321) |

These results are very similar to those of Experiment 6.
Tracing again has a very small effect on order memory, but
in this case it is slightly beneficial.   The effects of visual
interference on memory for order appear to be less marked
than motor interference, but again there is no suggestion of
a differential effect of interference in the different presentation conditions.

The correlations were subjected to an analysis of variance with presentation conditions and presence or absence
of interference as within subject variables and order of
conditions as between subjects variable.   Just one effect
reached an acceptable level of significance.   This was the
interaction between interference and order of presentation
conditions ($F = 4.32$; d.f. 1, 22; $p < 0.05$).   This interaction reflects the fact that interference impedes the retention of order information when the V condition is first, but
improves it slightly when the VT condition is first.   Once
again, however, the effects of order are not separable from
stimulus effects.

Interference did not significantly effect memory for order
($F = 1.40$; d.f. 1, 22; NS) and this, at least in part, may
be due to the lower level of interference produced by the
visual compared to the motor interference task.

Discussion

The results of this experiment support the interpretation of
Experiment 6.  The most important result in this respect is
the significant interaction between interference, presentation conditions and type of interference.  This shows that
the effects of visual and motor interference differ in the two
presentation conditions.  Motor interference is most disruptive in the VT condition, while visual interference tends to
be most disruptive in the V condition.  This pattern of
results provides strong evidence that the effects of interference in these experiments are modality specific and
would seem to rule out explanations in more general terms.
    There is little to say about the data on order memory
obtained here.  Once again tracing failed to improve memory
for order, which is consistent with previous results.  The
failure of visual interference to impair memory for order,
compared to the impairment in order memory produced by
the motor interference task in the previous experiment,
seems most easily explained in terms of the visual interference task being generally easier to perform.


GENERAL DISCUSSION AND CONCLUSIONS

Tracing around forms improves memory for them and the
experiments in this chapter provide support for the hypothesis outlined earlier, that this improvement depends on the
operation of a separate motor memory system.  The differential effects of motor interference as compared to the relatively uniform effects of visual interference on items memorised in the two conditions are clearly consistent with the
latter claim, and inconsistent with any simple attentional
explanation.  At the very least such effects demonstrate
that the memorised items are differently encoded in these
two conditions;  and these encoding differences are highly
consistent with the proposed mechanism.  The present
experiments also extend previous findings in showing that
tracing improves the visual recognition of non-verbal forms
in children of average ability, and also in adults.  Previous
studies have only found improvements in memory following
tracing in children retarded in their reading (Berman, 1939;
Ofman and Shaevitz, 1963;  Roberts and Coleman, 1958).
    Theoretically, tracing around a simple graphic form
demands that the subject perform a movement that completely

defines that form.   If remembered, such a movement
embodies all the information that is necessary to identify
the form.   The present experiments imply that this motor
information can summate in some way with information
stored about the form's visual appearance, so that at some
level of abstraction visual and motor information must share
a common representation.   This idea of an integrated
memory store in which visual and motor information are
both represented is not new.   Connolly and Jones (1970)
proposed just such a store to explain their results in a
visual-kinaesthetic matching experiment.   Diewert (1975)
in a short term motor memory study, employing visual and
motor interference, also suggested such a storage mechanism because memory for the location of a movement was
disrupted by both visual and motor interference.   From a
very different starting point, Meltzoff and Moore (1977)
found it necessary to postulate an innate common representation of visual and motor information to account for their
finding that infants can imitate facial gestures they see
others perform, but which they cannot have seen themselves
performing.   The present experiments are therefore consistent with others which imply that visual and motor
memories can share a common representation, but at the
same time show that storage of information from these different sensory modalities depends partly on sensory specific memory stores.

   This explanation of the effect of tracing in terms of the
summation of visual and motor information in memory recon-
ciles the present experiments, which show that tracing can
improve the recognition of abstract forms, and the experiments described earlier (p. 90), which indicated that
the addition of haptic information derived from palpating
abstract three-dimensional objects produced no such
improvement.   Such a discrepancy would be very difficult
to explain in terms of attention.   There seems no reason to
suppose that tracing a two-dimensional line form and palpating a three-dimensional object should differ in their
attention directing properties.

   This difference is explicable, however, in terms of the
information which is likely to be derived from these activities.   As pointed out earlier, tracing a two-dimensional
line form demands that the subject perform a movement
which completely defines that form.   In contrast, the
undirected palpating of three-dimensional objects would
provide only crude information about an object and there is

certainly  no guarantee that such information would completely specify the object.   So while in principle tracing
can give rise to a separate source of information which
could be used to recognise a form, there is reason to suppose that palpating a three-dimensional object would not
give rise to information which was complete enough to be
useful.

In addition to this, the type of information which could
potentially be encoded after palpating a three-dimensional
object is different to the motor information produced by
tracing.   Though difficult to specify precisely the information from palpating an object is presumably largely about
hand configuration and the tactual impression given by the
object.   It could be that such information is not encoded in
a way that enables it to summate with visual information in
memory in the way (according to the present theory) motor
information appears to do so.

This explanation of the effects of tracing on the visual
recognition of forms is also consistent with the explanation
given of the findings in Experiment 1.   While tracing
improved memory for letters in retarded readers it failed
to improve the normal readers' memory for letters.   This
failure of tracing to improve the normal readers' memory
for letters, it was argued, follows from their hypothesised
reliance on a phonological memory code.   Tracing is considered to improve memory for forms because an equivalent
source of motor information is encoded which also describes
the forms.   At some level of abstraction these separate
sources of information are presumed to have a common form
so that the motor information can combine with the visual
information to aid recognition.   Such a process cannot
occur for letters encoded phonologically, because there is
no sense in which the name of a letter and the movements
required to write it can be equivalent.

The experiments in the present chapter provide a further
demonstration that in these experiments tracing has consistently beneficial effects only on memory for items and not
their order.   This failure of tracing to aid order memory
is notable, especially since these experiments were prompted by the use of tracing as an aid to teaching children with
reading difficulties, and these children are often considered
to have particular difficulty with the ordering of letters in
words.   According to arguments advanced earlier, it seems
that the use of cursive script where a single integrated
motor programme is formed may be necessary for tracing to

aid memory for order.   If this is so, the absence of any improvements in order memory following tracing in the present experiments where discrete forms are used is quite reasonable.   Further studies will be necessary to clarify this.

The present results support the view implicit in Fernald's writing that tracing aids memory due to the production of a separate motor memory trace, and provide experimental evidence for the psychological processes postulated to underlie her remedial teaching method.

The existence of a distinct motor memory system which could aid visual memory was earlier proposed by William James (1890).   James refers to the use of tracing in teaching people to draw from memory, and an observation quoted by Galton, that a North American Indian, when shown a drawing, carefully followed its outline with his knife 'saying that this was to enable him to carve it out the better on his return home'.   Most interestingly for the present discussion, James also quotes reports of neurological cases who had lost the ability to read after cerebral injury, but who could read by tracing around the letters; this is attributed to the existence of a distinct motor memory system.

The motor image gives us the key to the problem.   If the patient can read, so to speak, with his fingers, it is because, in tracing the letters he gives himself a certain number of muscular impressions which are those of writing.   In one word, the patient reads by writing (Charcot): the feeling of the graphic movements suggests the sense of what is being written as well as sight would.

Similar cases are quoted by Goldstein (1948), Sasanuma (1974) and Gechswind (1965) who discuss their possible pathology.   Thus the explanation of the present findings is consistent with the ideas held by those who have used tracing as a mnemonic device in the past, and also gains some credence from cases of brain damage.   It is perhaps surprising that these ideas have existed for so long without experimental study.

In the next chapter we now turn to consider whether tracing may in certain circumstances aid memory for order or whether, as in the previous experiments, its effects are totally restricted to improving item memory.   This question is an interesting one theoretically, and also appears relevant to assessing the way in which tracing helps in remedial teaching.   Learning to read, and perhaps more so to spell, clearly involves remembering letter sequences, not just individual letters.   If tracing around words helps retarded readers learn to read and spell them because it acts as a memory aid, one might reasonably expect it to improve memory for the order of the letters in words as well as the letters themselves.

# 5 The effects of tracing on memory for order

INTRODUCTION

In the experiments reported in Chapters 3 and 4, tracing had consistently beneficial effects on the recognition of individual forms and, equally consistently, failed to have any effect on the subjects' memory for their order. This is puzzling. Tracing reputedly helps retarded readers learn to read and spell and this certainly requires memory for the order of letters within words. It seems reasonable to ask, therefore, whether tracing might also improve memory for order in circumstances which are more comparable to those in the remedial teaching situation. It is this issue which will be explored in the present chapter.

One obvious difference noted earlier between the situation in these experiments, and that of the teaching situation, is that in remedial teaching tracing is used in conjunction with words written in cursive script, whilst in these experiments strings of discrete letters and forms have been used. It seems reasonable to think that memory for order might be improved when tracing round a linked series of forms which allows the development of an integrated motor pattern. This is the idea which will be pursued in this chapter.

## EXPERIMENT 8. THE EFFECTS OF TRACING ON MEMORY FOR CURSIVE LETTER SEQUENCES

### Introduction

In the present experiment memory for cursive letter sequences was examined in children of normal reading ability. In

Experiment 1 tracing failed to have a significant effect on
memory for letters in normal readers.   The present experiment, it was hoped, would provide additional evidence relevant to this question.   In addition it seemed possible that
any effects of tracing on order memory might be at least
partially separable from those on item memory.

Method

The method employed is based on previous experiments, the
main difference being in the material used.
    (a)  Subjects.   Twenty children, seven boys and thirteen
girls from a village school near Oxford served as subjects.
They were drawn from a single class with the restriction
that all were said to be reading adequately according to
their class teacher.   The mean age of the sample was 9
years 2 months, with a range from 8 years 9 months to 9
years 7 months.
    (b)  Design.   A short term memory task was used in which
subjects attempted to remember a series of eight letters on
each of eight trials.   The experiment was split into two
blocks of four trials;  in one block the subject looked at the
letters (V condition) and in the other simultaneously traced
around them (VT condition).   Order of presentation conditions was counterbalanced across subjects.   Stimuli were
counterbalanced across conditions.
    (c)  Materials.   The materials consisted of the fourteen
consonants b, c, d, f, g, h, m, n, p, q, s, t, v and w.
Each letter was a photographically enlarged version of a
typewritten character produced by a Hermes typewriter with
a cursive script typeface.   All letters were enlarged by an
equal amount so that the tallest letter was 5 cm high.   A
set of fourteen letters was produced with each letter
centred on a separate 10 x 7.5 cm white print.   The eight
memory stimuli consisted of random letter sequences eight
letters long.   Each series was formed by typing the letters
adjacently to each other and the links between them were
touched in with black ink before the final photographic
enlargement was made.   This gave a series of eight letters
in cursive form which could be traced around by the subject
with continuous finger contact.   An example of one of the
letter sequences used is shown in Figure 4.   Each series
was printed on a 19 x 12.5 cm card.
    (d)  Procedure.   Subjects were tested individually in a

# *gpqsbhnt*

FIGURE 4  An example of one of the letter sequences used in Experiment 8

quiet room in their school, each session lasting approximately 30 minutes. During the session the experimenter and the subject sat side by side in front of a large table. A screen enabled the experimenter to manipulate stimuli and to record responses out of the subject's sight. No knowledge of results was given, but the experimenter encouraged subjects to maintain their interest and motivation.

The experiment was presented as a remembering game involving letters. Presentation of test trials was preceded by a demonstration trial in which a series of three letters was presented to the subject to remember. This trial was not scored and served to familiarise subjects with the procedure used throughout the experiment. The format of the three letter sequence used was identical to that of the eight letter sequences used subsequently. When the VT condition was first the subjects traced around the demonstration series of three letters and this was the only demonstration they received. For subjects who had the V condition first the act of tracing was demonstrated and practised by them immediately before the VT trials using the same series of three letters.

A serial memory task was used; on each trial a random series of eight letters was presented to be memorised in order. Memory was tested by a recognition/reconstruction procedure, the subject was presented with the set of fourteen individual letters and was required to pick out the eight letters and place them in a row in the same order as they had been presented. On V trials the subjects were required to point with their index finger and touch each letter in the series while simultaneously saying its name. On VT trials the subject mimicked the act of writing the letter sequence with the tip of his index finger of his writing hand, while simultaneously naming each letter as it was traced. In order to do this he was instructed to hold the card with one hand and then make a slow definite movement with his finger tip actually touching the plastic cover of the card.

On both types of trial the series was presented for 45 seconds. This was determined to be long enough for the subject to trace around the letter sequence without hurrying, and indeed was longer than subjects generally required. Subjects sometimes indicated that they had memorised the series before the end of the presentation period, and were then told to continue looking at the letters until they were covered up.

The children were timed with a stop-watch. In order to enable presentation time to be controlled the memory series were placed on the table in front of the subject covered by a card. When the subject was ready the experimenter uncovered the series and simultaneously started the stop-watch. After 45 seconds the experimenter placed the cover over the series and removed it from in front of the subject. A delay of 15 seconds followed. The set of fourteen letters was laid out in random order on a large card and covered with another card. This arrangement was then placed on the table in front of the subject; at the end of the delay period the experimenter removed the cover exposing the set of fourteen letters to the subject. The subject then took as long as desired to pick out the eight letters remembered and arrange them in order. The subjects were told always to pick out eight letters even if this necessitated guessing.

Results

The scoring of results was identical to that in previous experiments.

(a) Item memory. In each condition the maximum possible score was 32 (four trials with eight letters presented on each). The means and standard deviations for the number of letters correctly recognised in the two conditions are presented in Table 17.

This pattern of results is similar to that in previous experiments. As in the case of the normal readers in Experiment 1, the improvement in memory following tracing is very small.

The scores for letters correct were subjected to a 2-way

TABLE 17 The means and standard deviations for the number of letters correct in the two conditions of Experiment 8 (maximum possible score 32)

| V | VT |
|---|---|
| 25.95 | 26.70 |
| (2.31) | (2.68) |

(2 x 2) analysis of variance with presentation conditions a within subject variable and order of presentation conditions a between subjects variable. No effects in this analysis were significant. The largest effect was the trend towards a main effect of presentation conditions which was far from being significant ($F = 1.69$; d.f. 1, 18; NS).

(b) Order memory. Kendall's tau was calculated for performance on each trial and the value for the four trials within each condition were then averaged. The means and standard deviations of these correlations for the two conditions are shown in Table 18.

TABLE 18 Means and standard deviations of the correlations between order of correctly recognised letters and their order of presentation in the two conditions of Experiment 8

| V | VT |
|---|---|
| 0.71 | 0.70 |
| (0.185) | (0.216) |

These values are clearly nearly identical and any adcantage there is seems to lie in the V condition.

The correlations were subjected to an analysis of variance in the same way as the scores for items correct with presentation conditions a within subject variable and order of presentation conditions a between subjects variable. No effects in this analysis approached significance, including the main effect of presentation conditions ($F = 0.07$; d.f. 1, 18; NS).

Discussion

In this experiment no effects of tracing either on memory for individual letters or their order approached significance.

In Experiment 1 the improvement in memory for letters with normal readers was also insignificant and much less prominent than in the retarded readers. The present results might be taken as further evidence for the fact that tracing does not improve memory for letters in normal children. The explanation of this advanced earlier, in terms of the ubiquity of verbal memory codes was supported by informal observations during the present experiment. There was evidence of verbal memory coding by these children in the form of overt rehearsal and in silent articulatory lip movements.

It should be noted, however, that there were procedural differences between the present experiment and Experiment 1. In particular the retention interval used in the present experiment was much shorter than in Experiment 1. This may also have affected the results of the experiment.

The complete absence of any sign of improvement in order memory following tracing in the present experiment is disappointing in terms of the original hypothesis. It seems that this also may relate to the use of verbal memory codes in the present situation, making the use of tracing redundant. Before the idea that tracing can aid order memory is rejected, further experiments will be necessary. The most obvious next step appears to be to conduct a non-verbal analogue of the present experiment. This would eliminate the use of verbal coding, which seems to be the most likely reason for the absence of any effects of tracing on memory in this experiment.

EXPERIMENT 9.  THE EFFECTS OF TRACING ON MEMORY FOR CURSIVE ABSTRACT FORMS

Introduction

Experiment 8 failed to show any beneficial effects of tracing on either item or order memory and it was hypothesised that this may have been due to the use of verbal memory codes for the letters. In order to test this idea the present experiment uses an identical methodology except for the substitution of abstract cursive graphic forms which cannot be readily named.

Method

The method was essentially the same as in Experiment 8, except for the substitution of abstract graphic forms as stimuli.

(a) Subjects.   Twenty children, ten boys and ten girls, from two schools in the Oxford area served as subjects. They were all reading adequately according to their class teachers.   Their mean age was 8 years 11 months with a range from 8.0 years to 9 years 11 months.

(b) Design.   This was the same as in Experiment 8, except that just seven forms were presented on each of six trials.

(c) Materials.   The stimuli consisted of the same set of abstract forms used in previous experiments.   A set of fourteen forms was produced with each form drawn in black ink on the centre of a 12 x 7.5 cm white card.   The six memory series were drawn in cursive form on a 20 x 12.5 cm card.   These forms were half the size of those used in previous experiments.

(d) Procedure.   This was identical to Experiment 8 except that subjects could not name the forms as they did the letters.


Results

The scoring and analysis of results was identical to that in previous experiments.

(a) Item memory.   In each condition the maximum possible score was 21 (three trials with seven shapes presented on each).   The means and standard deviations of the number of forms correctly recognised in the two conditions are presented in Table 19.

TABLE 19 The means and standard deviations for the number of forms correctly recognised in the two conditions of Experiment 9 (maximum possible score 21)

| V | VT |
|---|---|
| 17.00 | 17.60 |
| (1.747) | (1.759) |

Again, and in this case most surprisingly, there is only a very slight improvement in memory following tracing.

An analysis of variance was performed on these results, with presentation conditions a within subject factor and order of presentation conditions a between subjects factor. No effects in this analysis reached an acceptable level of significance. The largest effect was the trend towards a main effect of presentation conditions, which as in Experiment 8 was far from being significant ($F = 1.85$; d.f. 1, 18; NS).

(b) Order memory. The means and standard deviations of the correlations for the two conditions are shown in Table 20.

TABLE 20 The means and standard deviations of the correlations between the order of correctly recognised items and their order of presentation in the two conditions of Experiment 9

| V | VT |
|---|---|
| 0.58 | 0.50 |
| (0.320) | (0.209) |

As in Experiment 8, the values for the two conditions are very similar with a slightly larger advantage in the V condition in the present experiment. These results were subjected to an analysis of variance with presentation conditions a within subject variable and order of presentation conditions a between subjects variable. Once again, no effects in this analysis were significant.

Discussion

These results are very disappointing in terms of the original hypothesis, that tracing around a series of cursive forms might lead to an improvement in memory for their order. Even more puzzling than this, however, is the complete failure of tracing to aid item memory as it did in previous experiments. There are three differences in the method employed in this experiment, compared to that in previous experiments where tracing did aid item memory. The forms were smaller in this experiment, they were drawn cursively on a single card, and the delay period between presentation and recognition was also much shorter in the present experiment.

It seems that one of these differences must be responsible for the failure of tracing to aid memory in the present experiment. A possible explanation for the present negative results appears to be the use of cursive forms. These forms were probably somewhat confusing to the children, since they sometimes displayed uncertainty when pointing to the forms as to where the boundaries between them were. This uncertainty also hampered tracing. Since the boundaries between forms were not delineated, and since it was often impossible to trace around successive forms without either lifting the finger or backtracking, the children were sometimes confused as to what to do. It seems reasonable to suppose that such confusion might interfere with the development of a clear motor pattern which could be remembered. Another possible factor is the smaller size of the forms. The less extensive movements made while tracing around these, in the absence of any confusion, may be less memorable.

EXPERIMENT 10. A REPLICATION OF EXPERIMENT 9 WITH DISCRETE FORMS

Introduction

To test the idea that confusion while tracing around the cursive forms in Experiment 9 was a critical factor in attenuating the beneficial effects of tracing on item memory, it was decided to run a further experiment which was identical in every way except for the use of discrete forms as stimuli.

Method

The design and procedure were identical to Experiment 9 except for the use of discrete memory stimuli. These were the same random series of forms used in Experiment 9, but here they were drawn separately, evenly spaced on a 51 x 13 cm card.

(a) Subjects. Eighteen children, ten boys and eight girls, from an Oxford school served as subjects. Their mean age was 9 years 10 months with a range from 9 years 6 months to 10 years 4 months.

Results

The scoring and analysis of results was identical to that in previous experiments.

(a) Item memory. In each condition the maximum score was 21. The means and standard deviations of the number of forms correctly recognised in the two conditions of Experiment 10 are presented in Table 21.

TABLE 21 The means and standard deviations for the number of forms correctly recognised in each condition of Experiment 10

| V | VT |
|---|---|
| 18.33 | 18.83 |
| (1.65) | (1.69) |

These results are almost identical to Experiment 9 except for the slightly higher overall level of performance, reflecting the fact that the children were nearly a year older in this experiment.

The scores for items correct were subjected to an analysis of variance with presentation conditions a within subject variable and order of presentation conditions a between subject variable. This analysis confirmed the impression given by the means in Table 21. No effects were significant including the very slight improvement in memory following tracing ($F > 1$).

(b) Order memory. The means and standard deviations for the correlations in the two conditions of Experiment 10 are shown in Table 22.

TABLE 22 Means and standard deviations of the correlations between the order in which correctly recognised forms were arranged and the order in which they were presented in each condition of Experiment 10

| V | VT |
|---|---|
| 0.75 | 0.70 |
| (0.249) | (0.288) |

These results are again very similar to those in Experi-

ment 9, except for the slightly higher overall level of performance.  The correlations were subjected to an analysis
of variance with presentation conditions a within subject
variable and order of presentation conditions a between subjects variable.  Once again no effects approached significance including the main effect of presentation conditions
$(F > 1)$.

Discussion

In this experiment tracing again failed to produce any
improvement in memory.  This leads us to reject the notion
that the major factor leading to the negative results in
Experiment 9 was the use of cursive forms which might be
confusing for the children.  This leaves the small size of
the forms used or the short delay period, as possible causes
of the negative results of Experiments 9 and 10.  The next
experiment examined whether the size of the forms was the
critical factor which had abolished the effects of tracing in
these experiments.

EXPERIMENT 11.   A REPLICATION OF EXPERIMENT 9
WITH LARGER MEMORY STIMULI

Method

This was identical in every way to that in Experiment 9,
except for the use of larger forms as stimuli.  They were
the same size as used in earlier experiments, i.e., twice
the size of those in Experiments 9 and 10, and were drawn
cursively.
   (a) Subjects.  Twelve children, seven girls and five
boys, whose mean age was 9 years 1 month (range from 8
years 5 months to 10 years 7 months) served as subjects.
They were seen at an Oxford school.

Results

The scoring of results was identical to that in previous
experiments.
   (a) Item memory.  The means and standard deviations
for the number of forms correctly recognised in the two
conditions are shown in Table 23.

TABLE 23 Means and standard deviations for the number of forms correctly recognised in the two conditions of Experiment 11

| V | VT |
|---|---|
| 16.5 | 16.9 |
| (2.195) | (2.274) |

Again it is apparent that tracing did not improve memory for the forms.

The scores for items correct were subjected to a 2-way (2 x 2) analysis of variance with presentation conditions a within subject variable and order of presentation conditions a between subjects variable. Once again no effects in this analysis were significant. The absence of a main effect of presentation conditions $(F > 1)$, confirms the impression given by Table 23 that tracing did not improve memory for the forms in this experiment.

(b) Order memory. The means and standard deviations of the correlations for the two conditions are shown in Table 24. Once again these values of tau are very similar in the two conditions.

TABLE 24 Means and standard deviations of the correlations between the order of correctly recognised forms and their order of presentation in the two conditions of Experiment 11

| V | VT |
|---|---|
| 0.54 | 0.67 |
| (0.299) | (0.255) |

The scores for the order in which the forms were arranged were subjected to a 2-way (2 x 2) analysis of variance with presentation conditions a within subject variable and order of presentation conditions a between subjects variable. No effects in this analysis were significant. Once again tracing had no significant effect on memory for order $(F = 1.92;$ d.f. 1, 10; NS$)$.

Discussion

Again in this experiment tracing had no reliable effects on
memory for the individual forms or their order.  We may,
therefore, also reject the notion that the small size of the
forms was the major cause of the negative results in Experiments 9 and 10.  This leaves the short delay used in these
experiments as the last possible explanation for the negative
results not yet examined.  This factor is examined in the
next experiment.


EXPERIMENT 12.  THE EFFECTS OF DELAY UPON THE
RECOGNITION OF FORMS FOLLOWING TRACING

Introduction

In the experiments reported earlier where tracing had a
beneficial effect on the recognition of forms, the delay
between stimulus presentation and recognition testing was
longer than that used in the experiments in the present
chapter.  In all the experiments reported in this chapter
the delay has been 15 seconds.  In the experiments in
Chapter 4, the delay period was either 1 minute 15 seconds,
or 1 minute 30 seconds.  During the experiments in Chapter
3, precise timing did not take place.  The delay there was
also necessarily much longer than the 15 seconds employed
in the present chapter, however, because in those experiments (1, 2 and 3) the experimenter gathered the forms or
letters presented to be memorised and thoroughly shuffled
them with the other forms or letters not presented, before
displaying the whole set of stimuli at recognition testing.
    These differences in the delay period, raise the possi-
bility that the beneficial effects of tracing on visual recognition depend critically upon the delay between stimulus
presentation and recognition testing.  In order to test this
idea, in the present experiment, memory for abstract forms
with tracing (VT) or without tracing (V) is again examined,
but in this case the delay between stimulus presentation and
recognition testing is varied.

Method

The details of the method are identical to those of previous
experiments except for the differences in design described
below.
     (a)  Subjects.   Sixteen children, seven boys and nine
girls, whose mean age was 9 years 1 month (range 8 years
8 months to 9 years 4 months) served as subjects.   They
were seen at an Oxford first school.
     (b)  Design.   The same short term memory task was used
as in previous experiments.   In this experiment there were
eight trials on each of which seven forms were presented to
be memorised in order.   Each series of seven forms was
drawn on a single 53 x 13 cm card.   The forms were drawn
separately and equally spaced on the card.   The experiment
was split into two blocks of four trials.   In one block the
child looked at the forms (V condition) and in the other simultaneously traced around them (VT condition).   In each
condition the memory stimuli were present for 45 seconds.
The length of delay between removal of the memory series
from the subjects' view and recognition testing was varied
within each of these presentation conditions.   On the middle
two trials there was a long delay (1 minute 30 seconds) and
on the first and fourth trial there was a short delay (15
seconds).   Order of presentation conditions was counterbalanced across subjects.   Half the subjects performed the
V condition first, and half had this condition second.   The
stimuli were counterbalanced across conditions, across
orders of conditions, and within each condition across the
long and short delay trials.


Results

The scoring of results was identical to that in previous
experiments.
     (a)  Item memory.   The means and standard deviations of
the number of items correct in the four conditions are shown
in Table 25.   These results are presented graphically in
Figure 5.
     It seems clear from this pattern of results that the length
of delay is critical in determining the effects of tracing on
memory.   At the short delay once again there is no beneficial effect of tracing; at the longer delay interval, however,
the beneficial effect of tracing is apparent.

TABLE 25  Means and standard deviations for the number of forms correctly recognised in each condition of Experiment 12

|     | Delay Short | Long |
| --- | --- | --- |
| V | 11.81 (1.328) | 10.06 (1.436) |
| VT | 11.75 (1.807) | 11.50 (1.506) |

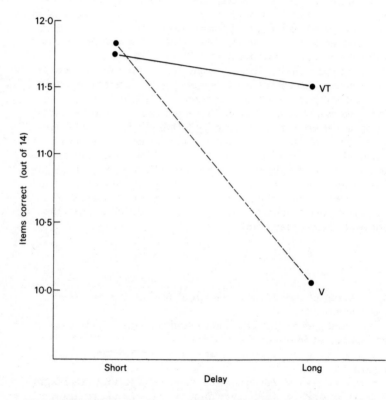

FIGURE 5  Mean number of items correct as a function of presentation conditions and length of delay in Experiment 12

The results were subjected to a 3-way (2 x 2 x 2) analysis of variance, with length of delay and presentation conditions as within subject variables and order of presentation conditions a between subject variable.

The main effect of presentation conditions showed that items were remembered better following tracing ($F = 5.33$; d.f. 1, 14; $p < 0.05$), and the main effect of delay showed that fewer items were remembered after the long delay ($F = 9.85$; d.f. 1, 14; $p < 0.01$).

Two interactions were also significant. The interaction of delay and presentation conditions showed that the length of delay did have a differential effect on memory in the two conditions ($F = 10.72$; d.f. 1, 14; $p < 0.01$). The means comprising this interaction were examined by the Tukey HSD test. This showed that at the long delay significantly more forms were remembered following tracing ($p < 0.01$) and that in the V condition significantly fewer items were recognised after the long delay ($p < 0.01$).

The interaction between presentation conditions and their order was also significant ($F = 7.44$; d.f. 1, 14; $p < 0.025$) indicating that the effect of tracing varied depending upon whether the VT condition was first or second. A Tukey test showed that this reflected the fact that tracing only produced a significant improvement in item memory when the VT condition was first ($p < 0.05$). This is consistent with the effects obtained in earlier experiments, but in this case we can be sure that this is a true effect of order, because here order is not confounded with stimuli as it was in earlier experiments.

(b) Order memory. As in previous experiments Kendall's tau was calculated for each trial and then averaged across trials within each condition. The means and standard deviations of the correlations for each of the four conditions are shown in Table 26.

Once again differences in memory for order between conditions are very small. The trend is for the order of items to be remembered better in the V condition, and most surprisingly, at the longer delay.

These correlations were subjected to an analysis of variance with presentation conditions and length of delay as within subject variables and order of presentation conditions a between subject variable. Not surprisingly, no effects in this analysis were significant.

TABLE 26 Means and standard deviations for the correlations between the order in which correctly recognised forms were arranged and the order in which they were presented in each condition of Experiment 12

|      | Delay | |
|      | Short | Long |
|------|-------|------|
| V    | 0.49 (0.369) | 0.53 (0.358) |
| VT   | 0.41 (0.244) | 0.50 (0.399) |

Discussion

The results of this experiment demonstrate that the length of delay between the presentation of items and recognition testing is critical to whether or not tracing improves performance. This provides an explanation for the absence of any effect of tracing in the previous experiments in this chapter, where a short delay was used.

It is clear from Figure 5, that while performance in the V condition declines rapidly during the delay, in the VT condition this decline is greatly reduced. While the short term retention of visual information appears to be susceptible to rapid decay (the term 'decay' is not used here in a theoretical sense as a cause of forgetting which is distinct from interference. It is merely used as a convenient description of the results obtained.) the addition of tracing appears to reduce this effect. In terms of the theoretical account of the effects of tracing on visual recognition given in Chapter 4 we might speculate that the addition of a motor memory trace either reduces the susceptibility of the visual trace to decay, or that as the visual trace decays the information in the motor trace being less susceptible to decay comes to be utilised more in the act of visual recognition.

At present it is not possible to elaborate these theoretical possibilities any further. The finding that the length of delay is a critical determinant of tracing's effects on visual recognition is certainly interesting and unexpected. It might also be interpreted indirectly, as further support for the theoretical account of the effect of tracing on visual recognition given in Chapter 4. This result certainly seems incompatible with an explanation of the effects of tracing cast solely in attentional terms, because there seems no reason to believe that an attention directing procedure would have less effect on memory over a 15 second, than a 1 minute 30 second, delay.

A question which immediately arises is whether this account of visual short term memory as a system susceptible to the fairly rapid loss of information is consistent with other research. There are difficulties in making comparisons here. All the experiments in this area have been with adult subjects and the procedures used have differed in several ways from that in the present experiment.

One approach to the study of short term visual memory with adults has relied on using forms which are complex and so preclude the use of verbal memory strategies. Phillips and Baddeley (1971) studied the time taken to recognise patterns comprised of a 5 x 5 matrix of squares each of which had a 50 per cent chance of being filled. Each pattern was presented for half a second and was followed by a pattern mask to eliminate the operation of iconic memory. After a delay of from 0.3 to 9 seconds a second matrix was presented. This was either identical or differed in one square from the original. The subject decided as quickly as possible whether or not the two patterns were the same. Both reaction time and errors increased over the delay, the decline in performance levelling out at 9 seconds. A subsequent experiment by Phillips (1974) using a similar procedure, examined memory for 4 x 4, 6 x 6, and 8 x 8 matrices. This showed that the rate of forgetting in this situation depended on stimulus complexity. Recognition of the 8 x 8 matrix patterns was at chance (50 per cent) level after 3 seconds while the 4 x 4 patterns were still well remembered (nearly 80 per cent correct) after 9 seconds.

These results are qualitatively similar to those of the present experiment in showing a rapid loss of information in visual short term memory, but the time span in these studies is much shorter than in the present experiment. There are, however, major differences in procedure between the experiments. In one case the subjects are adults, and in the other they are children. One requires very exact memory for a unique and complex pattern, the other requires recognition of a series of forms which are presented

repeatedly in different combinations.   In one case presentation was for half a second (Phillips and Baddeley, 1971)
or 1 second (Phillips, 1974) compared to 45 seconds in the
present experiment.   Clearly, with this multitude of differences between these experiments and the present one, little
can be said about any differences in time course for the loss
of information from short term visual memory.   At most we
might say there is a qualitative similarity:  both show evidence for a fairly rapid loss of information.

An alternative approach to the study of short term visual
memory in adults has examined memory for letters while
selectively interfering with verbal memory processes.   This
method has been developed by Kroll and his collaborators.

The first experiment of this type was by Kroll, Parks,
Parkinson, Bieber and Johnson (1970).   In this a single
letter was presented to be remembered, and then there followed a delay in which the subject had to shadow (repeat out
loud) a stream of spoken letters.   The memory letter was
presented either visually or aurally amongst the shadowed
letters spoken in a male rather than a female voice.   Recall
was much better for the visually presented letters at a 25
second delay interval.   Subjects also made more errors in
the shadowing task when trying to remember the auditory
letters.   This was interpreted as evidence for the visually
presented letters being remembered in visual terms.

A subsequent experiment explored this effect further
(Salzberg, Parks, Kroll and Parkinson, 1971) and examined
another prediction from the theory that the visual and auditory memory letters were stored separately.   This concerned the phonemic similarity of the memory letters to the
shadow letters.   It was predicted that if the auditory
letters were stored in some speech-like form then any similarity between the sound of the shadow and auditory memory
letters ought to interfere with performance.   Conversely,
if the visually presented letters were stored in a visual
form, then any similarity in sound between them and the
shadow letters should be irrelevant.   This prediction was
confirmed but only when the acoustically similar shadow
letters were presented within 4 seconds of the memory letter.

These two experiments clearly show that the visually presented letters are not being recoded into speech.   They do
not directly demonstrate that they are being retained in a
visual code, however.   The next experiment aimed to
demonstrate this.

This study (Parks, Kroll, Salzberg and Parkinson, 1972)

used a technique originally developed by Posner and Keele (1967), where subjects had to classify pairs of letters according to whether they both had the same name or not. In the Posner and Keele study letters which were physically identical as well as having the same name (e.g. A-A and a-a) were classified 'same' more quickly than pairs which were physically different (A-a) (the 'Posner' effect). This was only true for letter pairs presented within 1.5 seconds of each other, suggesting that the subject was changing from a match based on visual coding to one based on name coding. Parks et al. (1972) reasoned that if shadowing prevented the recoding of visual letters into a name code, then concurrent shadowing would lead to the preservation of the Posner effect at longer intervals. This prediction was confirmed; with concurrent shadowing 'same' letter pairs of the same case were matched faster than pairs with the same name but of different case at an 8 second delay interval. Subsequent experiments (Parks and Kroll, 1975) have questioned whether the loss of the 'Posner' effect at longer intervals in earlier experiments is attributable to a reliance on name codes. Rather it has been argued that it may be due to the generation of alternative visual memory forms. At any rate, these experiments show that single letters may be remembered in a visual form for at least 8 seconds.

Another experiment using a similar procedure to that of Parks et al. (1972) looked at same/different decisions about pairs of letters which as well as being either upper or lower case also varied in orientation (some pairs were mirror image letters) (Kellicut, Parks, Kroll and Salzberg, 1973). Once again there was an 8 second delay between letters during which subjects had to shadow aurally presented letters. As predicted the reversed letters were matched more slowly when the memory and test letters had the same name but differed in case, because the reversed letters were harder to read. Where the letters had the same case and the same name, being in a reversed orientation did not slow their classification as the same. This is therefore consistent with the idea that the same case letter pairs are matched solely in terms of visual features.

In summary, the experiment of Kroll et al. (1970) shows that a single visually presented letter can be retained for at least 25 seconds while shadowing other letters, and the subsequent experiments by this group indicate that performance in this situation depends upon the retention of a visual representation of the letter. Once again, however, the differences between these experiments and the present experiment are truly enormous, and any comparisons are fraught with difficulties. The Kroll et al. (1970) study provides evidence for the existence of a visual short term memory system which shows a loss of information between 10 and 25 second delay intervals. Unfortunately this group have not studied any longer retention intervals than this.

In conclusion, it appears that studies of visual short term memory in adults are methodologically so different from the present experiment that any detailed comparisons of findings is meaningless. The present experiment showed that visual short term memory for graphic forms in children declined sharply when the delay between stimulus presentation and recognition testing was lengthened from 15 seconds to 1 minute 30 seconds. The experiments on visual short term memory in adults reviewed here do not conflict with this finding. These experiments have differed in many ways from the present one, however, and most importantly the range of delays used in the present experiment do not appear to have been examined in any studies with adults. This highlights our poor understanding of the parameters governing the short term retention of visual information. Nevertheless it is of slight interest that, despite the great differences between the present experiment and those with adult subjects, they are qualitatively in agreement in showing a rapid loss of information from visual short term memory.

One other finding in this experiment which deserves mention is the interaction between presentation conditions and their order. This was found in some earlier experiments (Experiments 2 and 3) but in those cases the effects of order were confounded with stimulus effects. In the present experiment such confounding was eliminated and the interaction occurred again. We can therefore be sure that there is a genuine interaction between these two variables. The interpretation of this effect is quite straightforward. There is a trend for performance to decline over trails, while tracing has a beneficial effect on performance. When the VT condition is first performance in this condition is significantly better than in the V condition because the beneficial effects of tracing on memory summate with the tendency towards better performance on the earlier trials. Conversely, when the VT condition is second the improvement in performance due to tracing is masked by the tendency for performance to decline on later trials.

Finally, in considering the results on order memory, once

again there is little to say.   This experiment provides yet
a further demonstration that tracing does not improve memory
for order in this situation.


EXPERIMENT 13.   THE EFFECTS OF TRACING ON
MEMORY FOR CURSIVE ABSTRACT FORMS: A REPLICA-
TION OF EXPERIMENT 11 WITH A LONGER DELAY
INTERVAL

Introduction

In this experiment we return to the question of whether
tracing cursive forms can lead to an improvement in order
as well as item memory.   Given the finding that tracing is
only effective in aiding memory for forms at longer delay
intervals it seemed natural to examine the effects of tracing
cursive forms when using a long delay.


Method

This was the same as Experiment 11, except that the delay
between presentation and recognition testing was 1 minute
30 seconds and also in the present study stimuli were
counterbalanced across presentation conditions and order of
presentation conditions.
   (a)  Subjects.   Sixteen children, five girls and eleven
boys, from an Oxford first school served as subjects.
Their mean age was 9 years 1 month (range from 9 years 5
months to 8 years 3 months).


Results

The scoring of results was identical to that in previous
experiments.
   (a)  Item memory.   The means and standard deviations for
the number of forms correctly recognised in the two conditions are shown in Table 27.

TABLE 27 Means and standard deviations for the number of forms correctly recognised in each condition of Experiment 13

| V | VT |
|---|---|
| 15.94 | 17.13 |
| (2.144) | (1.821) |

As expected on the basis of previous experiments, it seems clear that more forms are recognised correctly following tracing.

The scores for items correct were subjected to a 2-way (2 x 2) analysis of variance with presentation conditions a within subject variable and order of presentation conditions a between subjects variable. This analysis showed that the improvement due to tracing was significant ($F = 5.32$; d.f. 1, 14; $p < 0.05$). No other effects were significant.

(b) Order memory. The means and standard deviations for the correlations for the two conditions are shown in Table 28.

TABLE 28 Means and standard deviations for the correlations between the order in which correctly recognised forms were arranged and the order in which they were presented in each condition of Experiment 13

| V | VT |
|---|---|
| 0.61 | 0.62 |
| (0.264) | (0.234) |

It is apparent that these two values are virtually identical. Once again, tracing does not appear to affect memory for order information.

The correlations were subjected to a 2-way (2 x 2) analysis of variance with presentation conditions a within subjects variable and order of presentation conditions a between subjects variable. This analysis confirmed the above interpretation; tracing did not have a significant effect on memory ($F = 0.077$; d.f. 1, 14; NS) and nor were any other effects significant.

## Discussion

As expected, given the long delay between stimulus presentation and recognition testing, tracing improved memory for the cursively drawn forms in this experiment.  The results on order memory were, however, most disappointing in terms of the hypothesis which prompted the experiment.  It was thought that tracing a cursive series of forms might lead to improvements in order as well as item memory. This hypothesis, however, received no support at all in this experiment.  Memory for order was essentially identical in the V and VT conditions.  This result is all the more marked given the clear effects of tracing on item memory obtained here.

It must be concluded that any effects of tracing on order memory are less robust than its effects on item memory. Obviously, however, the null hypothesis – that tracing cannot improve order memory – cannot be proved.  It might be that in other circumstances tracing does improve memory for order.

It is clear that many skills involve complex series of movements which must be remembered in their correct serial order.  Driving is one example of such a skill.  Of more relevance to the present discussion is writing. Skilled writing involves the performance of complex serially organised movements.  When writing common words the movements are quite automatic, as for example, when signing one's name.

These examples have an indirect relevance to the present discussion.  Tracing appears to improve memory for forms due to the encoding of motor information (Chapter 4).  Consideration of skilled writing suggests that the motor memory system is capable of encoding sequential information; because of this it remains theoretically reasonable to suppose that tracing around a series of forms might improve memory for their order as well as memory for the forms themselves.

The fact remains that in the present experiments no evidence for tracing improving order memory has been found. The negative results in this respect of the present experiment demonstrate that this failure is not due, as originally suggested, to the use of discrete forms.  If tracing words in the remedial teaching situation does have any effects on memory for the order of letters, this must reflect some other difference between the present experiment and the teaching situation.  From considering writing patterns one obvious possibility is that such an effect might depend on repeating the movement pattern many times, possibly when distributed over long periods of time.

It is not known of course whether tracing words during remedial teaching does have dual effects on memory for the letters and their order.  It could be that the effects on item memory detected in the present series of experiments are the only ones operating.  Nevertheless, the possibility that tracing might improve order as well as item memory seemed interesting and worth pursuing experimentally.  A positive result in this regard in the present experiment would have been interesting theoretically, and practically, in terms of our understanding of these remedial teaching procedures. The negative results obtained must necessarily remain inconclusive.

## GENERAL DISCUSSION AND CONCLUSIONS

The overall results of the experiments in this chapter are rather negative.  The search for an effect of tracing on order memory had completely negative results.  Whether or not tracing can improve order memory in some situations remains an open question, but one which, because of the potential cost of research effort, did not seem worth pursuing further.

More positively, a variation in the length of delay between presentation of the nonsense forms and recognition testing, proved to have marked effects.  Originally this variation was introduced partly for experimental convenience and partly in an attempt to assess the generality and robustness of the effects of tracing on item memory.  The disappearance of the effect of tracing on visual recognition in the early experiments in this chapter led to Experiment 12. This demonstrated that the improvement in visual recognition following tracing was only true when a long (1 minute 30 seconds) but not a short (15 seconds) delay intervened between stimulus presentation and recognition testing.  The pattern of results in this experiment was quite unexpected, and indicated that there was a fairly rapid loss of information from visual short term memory across the delay intervals studied.  Such a decline in performance could not have been predicted from previous studies of visual short term memory, and underlines the incompleteness of knowledge in

this area.   A further problem raised by these experiments
is why the effects of delay are so much less marked following
tracing.   In terms of the theory advanced in Chapter 4, a
likely explanation might be in terms of the motor memory
trace being more durable than the corresponding visual
trace.

In the next chapter we return to a paradox raised in
Chapter 3.   The present series of experiments have shown
that tracing can improve visual recognition.   Conversely,
it appears that most retarded readers who are reputedly
helped to learn to read by tracing around words, do not
suffer from visual memory problems.   Rather, they appear
to have verbal memory problems.   In the next chapter,
therefore, we examine whether tracing has any effects on
the learning of verbal labels for visual configurations.   If
such an effect occurred it would provide a likely explanation
for the beneficial effects which tracing is claimed to have in
the remedial teaching of retarded readers.

# 6 Experiment 14: the effects of tracing on visual-verbal paired associate learning

## INTRODUCTION

The pattern of results in the previous series of experiments presents something of a paradox. On the one hand the majority of retarded readers do not show evidence of any visual perceptual or memory problems (pp. 21-32) but they do have verbal memory problems (pp. 45-52) and Experiment 1). On the other hand, earlier experiments have shown that tracing, as used to teach these children to read, aids visual recognition. If retarded readers have normal visual memory abilities why should a procedure which improves visual recognition help them? According to the evidence presented in Chapter 1, their problem in learning to read is unlikely to be one of remembering the visual configurations of words, but rather one of learning the verbal labels of these configurations. It is not immediately clear how a procedure which improves visual recognition could improve verbal associative learning such as is involved in learning to read. It is this paradox which will be considered here.

One possible solution to this paradox is in terms of reading strategies. In Experiment 1 the retarded readers appeared to rely more on a visual memory strategy than did the normal readers when memorising letters. This difference might also extend to reading, the retarded readers again relying more on a visual strategy. There is one tenuous piece of evidence that this is so. Boder (1973) reported that retarded readers sometimes make semantically related errors such as reading 'funny' for 'laugh', which are comparable to the errors made by brain damaged adults with 'deep' or 'phonemic' dyslexia. Bryant and Bradley (1980) mention a similar example of a retarded reader who when asked to read the word 'pasteurised' said 'well, you boil it'.

144

Work with phonemic dyslexic patients has sought to explain these bizarre semantic errors which occur in their reading, in terms of models of the normal reading process. It has been suggested in several reports that the basic deficit in these patients (or one of the basic deficits) is an inability to convert printed words into a phonological form (Shallice and Warrington, 1975; Saffran and Marin, 1977; Marcel and Patterson, 1977).

The most formal statement of this is by Marcel and Patterson (1977). According to their model, reading (single words) consists of the reader accessing the meaning of the printed word in a sort of internal dictionary. There are two routes to this dictionary. One depends upon a direct access to the meaning of the word from its visual appearance. An alternative is an indirect route which involves the translation of the printed word into a phonological representation which is then used to access the dictionary. It is proposed that in the phonemic dyslexic this second phonological route to meaning is impaired. It may be that these patients have other abnormalities in their lexical-semantic system also. These further elaborations and the detailed evidence upon which this model is based will not be dealt with here. The important point for the present discussion is the persistent suggestion that they read by a direct visual route from print to meaning. Since the retarded readers may show certain similarities to phonemic dyslexics by making semantic errors in reading, and finding words of high imagery value easier to read than those of low imagery value (see below), an interesting possibility is that in reading they also rely more on a visual route from print to meaning. If this were so tracing might help them by improving the quality of their visual memory for words.

A possibly more plausible, but not contradictory explanation of the beneficial effects of tracing, in teaching retarded readers, comes from a consideration of the association of written and spoken language. This was prompted by an observation of an experienced remedial teacher of retarded readers, who routinely used tracing as a teaching aid for these children. She remarked that some severely retarded readers have persistent difficulties in learning the names of the individual letters of the alphabet, and that having these children trace around the outline of letters while saying the name was a particularly effective way of overcoming this problem. Repeated experience of simultaneously saying and

tracing individual letters apparently helped these children
remember the letter names.   This seemed to be a particularly clear example of the visual-verbal paired associate
learning difficulty which has been shown to be characteristic
of retarded readers (p. 52).   It also strongly suggested
that tracing may be an aid to such learning.   In a similar
vein Fernald and Keller (1921) while discussing the success
of their tracing procedure in teaching retarded readers,
talk of kinaesthetic cues from tracing and pronouncing the
word helping the child to associate its written and spoken
forms.

In a very simple model one might consider learning to read
as a paired associate learning task in which a name has to be
associated with the visual stimulus of the printed word.
This description may be particularly apt in the case of retarded readers who teachers often describe as being peculiarly
insensitive to the rules governing written language.   They
often appear to treat each new word as a unique entity with
no relationship to other words in their vocabulary.   This
may depend on their inability to perceive similarities between
like sounding words which they can hear and repeat (Bradley
and Bryant, 1978) and also perhaps their difficulty in segmenting speech into syllables and phonemes (Liberman et al.,
1977; Savin, 1972).   Such difficulties would lead to words
being treated as wholes because of an inability to understand
the rule governed nature of our alphabetic writing system.
They would also cause difficulties in decoding a printed word
into a representation in sound, and so favour reading by a
visual route.

There are two independent pieces of evidence that support
the idea that retarded readers do indeed tend to rely on a
whole word strategy when reading which for them makes
reading comparable to paired associate learning.   Bradley
and Bryant (1979) showed that children sometimes spell
words that they fail to read, and this occurs more often in
retarded readers than amongst normals of the same reading
age.   This relative independence of reading and spelling in
the retarded readers was interpreted in terms of their
reliance on a letter by letter strategy when spelling but a
visual whole word strategy when reading.

The other piece of evidence concerns the imagery value of
words.   Jorm (1977) showed that high imagery words were
easier to read for children retarded in their reading (as
they are for adult brain damaged dyslexic patients (Richardson, 1975a, 1975b)) but not for normal readers.   This was

also related to the retarded readers reading by a whole word method, and the fact that in verbal paired associate learning the imageability of a word has been found to predict ease of learning (Paivio, 1971). In a further experiment good and poor readers were forced to use a whole word strategy by having them learn to read words represented by abstract shapes in a paired associate learning paradigm. In this case, as expected, imageability was related to ease of learning in both groups.

Paired associate learning seems a reasonable model for learning to read at least in the early stages and perhaps particularly for retarded readers. There is also evidence, however, that these children are bad at PAL tasks with a verbal component such as reading (p. 52). This together with the observations above prompted the idea that tracing around a written word may aid the association of its written and spoken forms.

It is known that redundant stimulus cues facilitate paired associate learning (Trabasso and Bower, 1968). For example, learning to associate nonsense syllable pairs occurs more quickly if one set of syllables is printed on cards of different colours compared to when all syllables occur on the same grey background (Weiss and Margolius, 1954). Tracing might have a similar effect. A word which is traced around will, according to previous results, have a dual representation in memory in terms of visual and motor memory traces (Chapter 4). This is also a form of stimulus redundancy comparable, perhaps, to a set of words occurring on distinctively coloured backgrounds.

With these considerations in mind the present experiment examines the effects of tracing on visual-verbal paired associate learning. Children of average ability learned names for abstract shapes which were either traced around or looked and pointed at. It was felt that this situation provided an approximation to the early stages of learning to read comparable to the retarded readers early remedial teaching experiences.


METHOD

(a) Subjects. Twenty children, nine girls and eleven boys, from an Oxford school participated in the experiment. Their mean age was 9 years 1 month (range 8 years 2 months to 9 years 8 months).

(b) Materials.  The stimuli consisted of ten abstract shape triplets.  The shapes were the same as those used in previous experiments.  Each triplet of shapes was drawn in black ink on a 20 x 13 cm white card which was protected by a plastic cover.

Each triplet was paired with a noun of high frequency (AA count in Thorndike-Lorge) and high imagery value (rating between 6 and 7 on the Paivio, Yuille and Madigan, 1968, norms).  The ten noun shape pairs were split into two groups of five.  The nouns of each group had equal imagery ratings (averages of 6.69 and 6.67).

(c) Design.  The task was for the child to learn the name which was paired with each of the ten shape triplets. There were two presentation conditions, visual (V) and visual plus tracing (VT).

There were eight study test trials, four on the five shape triplet noun pairs presented in the V condition and four on the shape triplet noun pairs presented in the VT condition. V and VT study test trials alternated.  The order of presentation conditions was counterbalanced across subjects and stimuli were counterbalanced across presentation conditions and their order.  On each study or test trial items were presented in a different order to prevent serial learning.

(d) Procedure.  Subjects were tested individually in one session lasting approximately 30 minutes.  They were told that there was a series of shape triplets on cards and that they were going to learn the name which went with each shape triplet.

Each triplet was shown to the subject for 15 seconds.  As a triplet was presented the experimenter said 'The word ___ goes with these shapes.'  In the V condition the subject pointed to each of the three shapes in turn simultaneously saying the appropriate name aloud.  The VT condition was identical except that the subject traced around each shape in turn with the tip of his index finger instead of pointing.

After each presentation of five triplets retention of the names was tested.  The subject was shown each of the shape triplets in turn and asked to say the appropriate name. When incorrect responses and refusals occurred the experimenter said the correct name.  Subjects were told when they gave the correct name, and praised for doing so.

RESULTS

The means and standard deviations for the number of shape
triplets correctly named on each trial in each condition are
shown in Table 29. This pattern of results is illustrated
graphically in Figure 6.

TABLE 29 Means and standard deviations for the number of
shape triplets correctly named on each trial in each condition of Experiment 14 (maximum possible score on each trial
= 5)

|     | 1 | 2 | 3 | 4 |
| --- | --- | --- | --- | --- |
| V | 2.15<br>(1.268) | 2.55<br>(1.190) | 2.40<br>(1.231) | 2.85<br>(1.424) |
| VT | 3.05<br>(1.317) | 2.80<br>(1.056) | 3.50<br>(0.946) | 3.65<br>(1.137) |

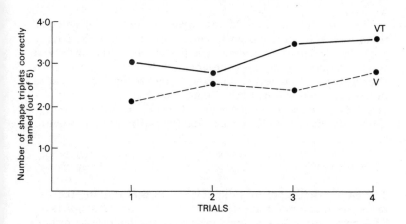

FIGURE 6 Mean number of shape triplets correctly named
on each trial in each condition of Experiment 14

It seems clear from these results that the names of the
shape triplets which were traced around are remembered
better.

The scores for correct responses were analysed in a 3-way (2 x 4 x 2) analysis of variance. Presentation conditions (V or VT) and trials (1 - 4) were within subject variables and the order of presentation conditions was a between subjects variable.

In this analysis the main effect of presentation conditions was significant (F = 12.55; d.f. 1, 18; p< 0.01) confirming that the names were remembered better for the triplets that had been traced around. The main effect of trials was also significant (F = 4.39; d.f. 3, 54; p < 0.01). A Tukey HSD test showed that performance on trial 4 was better than on trial 1 or 2 (p< 0.05).

Order of presentation conditions was not a significant factor but two interactions with this factor were. The effect of tracing varied with the order of conditions (F = 8.77; d.f. 1, 18; p < 0.01). A Tukey HSD test showed that when the V condition was first tracing did not significantly improve performance but when the V condition was second tracing did improve performance (p < 0.05). Performance in the first condition tended to be better than in the second; in the one case this trend operated to mask the beneficial effects of tracing, while in the other it summated with it.

The interaction of trials with order of presentation conditions was also barely significant (F = 2.82; d.f. 3, 54; p < 0.05). This variation in the pattern of learning across trials, depending on the order of presentation conditions is illustrated in Figure 7. In this figure group 1 consists of those subjects who had the V condition first, and group 2 consists of those subjects who had the VT condition first. This pattern of results is not readily explicable, however.


DISCUSSION

The major finding of this experiment is that tracing facilitates the learning of arbitrary names for visual symbols. This provides a likely explanation for the beneficial effects of tracing in the remedial teaching of retarded readers. According to the arguments presented in the Introduction, it appears that learning to read, especially in the case of retarded readers, involves paired associate learning of the sort examined in the present experiment. In addition, studies have shown that retarded readers are poor at such learning tasks. A procedure which facilitates this type of learning would therefore be likely to help them learn to read.

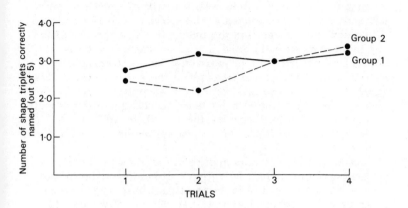

FIGURE 7 Mean number of shape triplets correctly named on each trial as a function of the order of presentation conditions in Experiment 14

The theoretical question of how to account for tracing's facilitation of visual-verbal paired associate learning remains. The most obvious explanation comes from a consideration of earlier experiments where tracing was shown to improve visual recognition. In order to learn to associate a visual stimulus with a verbal label it is clearly necessary to recognise the visual stimulus. The importance of a stimulus recognition phase in paired associate learning was demonstrated in a verbal task by Martin (1967).

In Martin's experiment subjects were required to learn the digit which was paired with each of eight consonant trigrams. In an alternating sequence of aurally presented, study and test trials, eight pairs of trigrams and digits were presented on each of the study trials. During the test trials, however, twenty-four trigrams were presented, consisting of the eight old stimuli plus a set of sixteen new trigrams (a different set of sixteen new trigrams were used for each test trial). On the test trials, as each stimulus was heard the subject pressed one of two buttons, depending upon his decision as to whether the trigram had been presented before, or whether it was new. He then gave the digit paired with that trigram if it was old, or guessed a digit if the trigram was new.

Using this procedure, independent measures were taken on successive trials of how well the stimuli were recognised and how well the responses to the stimuli were remembered. Given correct recognition the proportion of correct responses increased steadily across trials, whereas without correct recognition the proportion of correct responses remained at chance level throughout the experiment. This shows that a prerequisite for paired associate learning to occur is that the subject must learn to recognise the stimuli. If a subject fails to recognise the stimuli he will also necessarily fail to learn the responses which are paired with them.

This same process also apparently applies to visual-verbal paired associate learning. It has been shown that the use of pictures of objects as stimuli in paired associate tasks produces faster learning than the use of words which represent the same objects. (For example a response paired with a picture of a tree will be learnt more quickly than if it is paired with the word tree, e.g. Paivio and Yarmey, 1966.) Wicker (1970) investigated this effect using the methodology developed by Martin (1967) with verbal materials. From this experiment it appeared that the faster rate of learning with pictures as stimuli depended on them being more easily recognised. Pictures were correctly recognised more often than the corresponding words. Moreover, when recognition was equal for pictures and words there was no difference in the probability of correctly recalling the response to either type of stimulus.

This line of reasoning provides a parsimonious explanation for the beneficial effects of tracing on visual-verbal paired associate learning found here. Tracing has been shown in previous experiments to improve visual recognition. From the above studies it appears that such an improvement would be expected to facilitate learning the names paired with these stimuli, because a necessary condition for such associative learning is that the visual stimuli be recognised.

These arguments certainly provide a parsimonious explanation for the experimental findings obtained here; but this explanation does not appear to resolve the paradox with which this chapter started. In terms of the present discussion this paradox can now be slightly rephrased. The retarded readers' difficulty in learning to read is unlikely to be one of remembering the visual configuration of words, but rather one of remembering the words' verbal labels.

Yet according to the above arguments the observed effects of tracing on visual verbal paired associate learning can be explained in terms of tracing facilitating the recognition of the visual stimulus.  However, this is precisely the aspect of the task with which we should expect the retarded reader to cope adequately.  If this were the only effect of tracing in this situation, we would not expect tracing to be of any special help to the retarded reader in learning to read.

Given the evidence reviewed earlier for a verbal memory problem amongst retarded readers, we might expect that if tracing were to be of particular help to them in learning to read it would need to have an effect on the verbal memory component of visual-verbal paired associate learning.

During the course of the experiment one observation strongly suggested that tracing was having such an effect. It appeared that the names associated with items presented in the VT condition often occurred as intrusive responses while the retention of the names of items presented in the V condition was being tested.  Intrusions of the opposite type seemed very much rarer, however.  It seemed that tracing improved retrieval of the names which were associated with it, making them generally more available as responses. Unfortunately no systematic recording of intrusion errors was made during this experiment, because this idea only evolved as a result of observing several subjects during the study.

This second explanation must obviously remain a tentative one.  It should be noted, however, that it is not incompatible with the previous explanation in terms of stimulus learning.  It is possible that tracing has effects on both visual stimulus learning and verbal response retrieval in this situation.  The answer to whether either, or both, of these mechanisms are in fact responsible for the observed effect of tracing on paired associate learning must await further research.


## SUMMARY AND CONCLUSIONS

The situation in the present experiment is obviously different to that encountered by the retarded reader learning to read.  The present situation is, however, at least closer to the teaching situation than were the experiments with which we began.  Imperfections in the match between these two situations are, it is felt, compensated for by the degree of control which it was possible to exercise in the present experiment.

The most important finding of this experiment was that tracing facilitated the learning of arbitrary names which were paired with a series of abstract patterns. This finding could not have been confidently predicted on the basis of any previous experiments, and provides further evidence to suggest that remedial teaching procedures which incorporate tracing are soundly based. This is particularly important given the arguments advanced, which suggest that the present experimental situation is similar to that in the early stages of learning to read.

The precise mechanisms responsible for the effect obtained and the way in which they relate to the retarded readers' demonstrated verbal memory problems remain open to some speculation. Two possible general mechanisms were advanced, but before their validity can be assessed further experiments are required. In this respect our understanding of the detailed mechanisms responsible for tracing's putative success as a remedial teaching aid for retarded readers remains incomplete. At least, however, the present experiment provides a base from which future studies of this can start. If we do not have any precise answers to the questions with which we began, at least we are now in a position to ask some more precise questions.

# 7 Summary, conclusions and implications

## INTRODUCTION

It seems appropriate, in this final chapter, to attempt a synthesis of the major points which emerge from the work reviewed at the beginning of this book, and from the experiments reported subsequently which pursued some of the questions posed there. Inevitably many questions remain unanswered. Hopefully, this reflects the fact that as knowledge accrues, more specific questions are asked. So for example, given the finding presented in Chapter 6, that tracing can improve visual-verbal paired associate learning, questions arise as to the mechanisms responsible for this effect, and about how these may relate to the problems of retarded readers. In this sense the proliferation of questions arising from much research, including the present work, is not a negative trend. In the course of this chapter some of the further questions raised by the present experiments will be outlined.

## THE CAUSES OF READING RETARDATION

From the research reviewed in Chapter 1 it seems unlikely that all cases of reading retardation have a common cause. In particular it appears that a likely cause for the majority of cases is some form of language impairment and verbal learning difficulty. There may also be another smaller group, however, for whom a visual memory impairment is the problem.

Experiments examining these issues have frequently ignored this possible heterogeneity. Although findings

155

concerning the visual perceptual and memory abilities of
this group are often contradictory, there is no good evidence
for retarded readers being generally poor on visual tasks.
Most importantly, those experiments whose visual memory
requirements were most similar to reading showed no difference between normal and retarded readers.  It remains
possible, however, that reports which only consider mean
differences between groups conceal a small group of retarded readers for whom such problems are important.  In
contrast, the oral language and verbal memory skills of
retarded readers do appear to be consistently worse than
those of controls.

The results of Experiments 1, 2 and 3 were essentially
in agreement with these previous findings.  The verbal
memory abilities of the retarded readers, as assessed in a
task requiring memory for series of letters, were worse
than those of the normal readers.  In contrast the two
groups performed at an equivalent level on an exactly comparable task involving memory for non-verbal forms.  The
scores for individual subjects were examined for evidence
that there may be a sub-group of retarded readers whose
problems stem from poor visual memory abilities.  None
was found.  This negative finding is not particularly compelling in so far as there were only twenty retarded readers
participating in this experiment.  It does suggest, however,
in agreement with other findings (see pp. 19-20) that visual
memory problems are probably not a common cause of reading retardation.

To turn to a consideration of the questions posed by these
results, three major possibilities will be mentioned here.
The first concerns the effectiveness of phonological STM
coding in retarded readers.  In order to explain the results
of Experiments 1, 2 and 3 it was postulated that the retarded
readers were deficient in the use of such memory codes.
This same idea has been proposed in other work (see pp.
49-51), but further evidence is certainly needed on this
question.

One particularly appealing approach to this problem would
be to try and demonstrate that retarded readers rely more
on a visual STM code than normal children.  This hypothesis was proposed to account for the results of Experiments
1, 2 and 3 and would seem a natural alternative if indeed
retarded readers are impaired in their ability or propensity
to use a phonological STM code.

A simple and ingenious method for demonstrating visual

STM coding was developed by O'Connor and Hermelin (1973).
In this experiment children were shown three visually presented digits which were exposed successively in three
windows, in such a way that the left to right order never
corresponded with the temporal-sequential order.   When
asked to recall these digits, normal children responded in
terms of temporal order.   Deaf children on the other hand
recalled in terms of the spatial (left to right) order.   This
pattern of results appeared consistent with the notion that
the normal children encoded the digits in an auditory-
temporal fashion, while the deaf remembered them in a
visual spatial form.   It would be interesting to apply this
procedure to retarded readers.   In so far as they are
reluctant to use a phonological STM code they might be
expected to perform in a similar way to deaf children in
this situation.

(A variant of this procedure was applied to the normal and
retarded readers who participated in Experiments 1 and 2.
In this case the digits were written on cards which were
placed face down on a table.   The experimenter then showed
the digits to the subject by turning the cards over one at a
time in such a way that the spatial and temporal orders did
not coincide.   All the subjects performed as if they were
deaf! There was an overwhelming tendency for all the
children, whether normal or retarded readers, to respond
in a spatially organised recall order.   This is obviously
not a serious failure to replicate the O'Connor and Hermelin
study, since the manner of presentation used was quite different, and in particular was much slower.   It was apparent, however, that this crude version of the procedure
would not demonstrate any possible differences in memory
coding, as originally hoped.   A precise replication of the
O'Connor and Hermelin study with normal and retarded
readers would seem worth while.)

An alternative approach to this problem might be to look
for visual confusion errors in the recall of letters or digits,
amongst retarded and normal readers.   If retarded readers
do rely more on a visual memory code than do normals for
remembering such materials, their recall profiles might
reveal a distinctive pattern of confusion errors based on
visual similarity.   Also the recall of retarded readers
might be more adversely affected by the use of lists of visually similar items than that of normal readers.   This
strategy is essentially that of applying the principles which
Conrad (1964; Conrad and Hull, 1964) used to demonstrate

phonological coding in short term memory for verbal materials. Such a strategy also raises a further theoretical issue as to whether the principles governing verbal STM also apply to the visual STM system.

A second larger issue, highlighted by the work reported here is the need to obtain better evidence for the existence of the group of retarded readers whose problems are thought to depend upon visual memory deficiencies. A possible starting point for such a study would be to examine the ability of retarded readers to copy, after a delay, fairly complex words. The task used in Experiment 2, would also appear likely to be sensitive to the problems of this group. It would also seem fruitful to unite experimental studies of this sort, with an examination of the spelling errors of these children, since Boder (1973) has claimed that retarded readers with visual problems make distinctive types of spelling errors. It would appear advisable for studies here to examine fairly large groups of retarded readers in view of the concensus of evidence indicating that such children are probably quite rare (pp. 19-20).

A third area of study which appears a promising one for understanding the problems of retarded readers is that of long term verbal memory. There is ample evidence (pp. 45-51 and Experiment 1) that retarded readers perform poorly on tests of short term verbal memory. Learning to read, however, involves long term verbal memory processes operating over extended time periods. Apart from paired associate learning studies there do not seem to be any studies of long term verbal memory in retarded readers. Further studies in this area are badly needed. The possibility exists that retarded readers may perform even more poorly in such tests than they do in tests of short term verbal memory.


THE USE OF TRACING IN TEACHING RETARDED READERS

The predominant objective of this work has been to explore, in an experimental situation, the use of tracing as a teaching aid for retarded readers. There is considerable faith amongst experienced remedial teachers that tracing is an effective teaching aid, and the work reviewed in Chapter 2 showed that these methods gained limited support from a few controlled studies. The effects of tracing found in the memory tasks used here provide further indirect support for the use of these methods.

In Experiment 1 it was shown that in a short term memory task involving series of letters tracing improved the performance of retarded, but not of normal readers. A likely explanation of this seemed to be in terms of the retarded readers' reliance on a visual, rather than a verbal, memory strategy. In agreement with this, in Experiment 2 where non-verbal forms were the stimuli, normal and retarded readers gained equal benefit from tracing the forms. Subsequent experiments explored the mechanisms responsible for this effect of tracing on visual recognition. Motor and visual interference tasks had a differential effect on memory for forms which had been looked at or looked at and traced around, and from this it was concluded that the effects of tracing on visual recognition depended upon the operation of a distinct motor memory trace. According to this view information in memory from the tracing movements summates with visual information about the forms, and serves to improve visual recognition.

Another series of experiments explored whether tracing could improve order as well as item memory. These experiments were negative. While tracing consistently improved the recognition of individual forms, it was never shown to improve order memory. Such effects might exist without having been detected. These experiments certainly show, however, that the effects of tracing on memory for items are more robust than are any possible effects on memory for order.

An incidental finding from the above series of experiments was that the delay between stimulus presentation and recognition testing was found to be a critical determinant of the effects of tracing on visual recognition. Tracing only improved recognition with a long delay (1 minute 30 seconds) but not with a short (15 seconds) one. This result was quite unexpected, but of theoretical interest because it implied that the hypothetical motor memory trace responsible for the improvements in visual recognition following tracing, was relatively more durable than the visual memory trace.

A final experiment explored the effects of tracing on visual-verbal paired associate learning. Tracing improved this. This is of interest because of the similarities between this situation and the early stages of learning to read. Learning the names and sounds of letters, and also quite probably the acquisition of a basic sight vocabulary, are examples of visual-verbal paired associate learning.   This finding provides a rationale for any beneficial effects of tracing in remedial teaching, and also an experimental paradigm in which such effects can be further explored.

This series of experiments has in some sense considerably increased our understanding of these remedial teaching procedures.   Tracing has demonstrable effects on memory; this increases our faith in these methods, and gives us indications as to how they may work.   At the same time, there remain gaps in our understanding.

A detailed problem which remains is how the effects of tracing on memory may relate to the causes of the retarded readers' difficulties.   According to the evidence presented in Chapters 1 and 3 the problems experienced by retarded readers in learning to read are unlikely to be in remembering the visual configurations of words but rather in learning the verbal labels of these visual configurations.   On the other hand, the experiments reported here have demonstrated that tracing, as used to teach these children to read, improves visual recognition.   If most retarded readers do not suffer any impairment of visual memory, it is not clear why a procedure which improves visual recognition should help them learn to read.   The effects of tracing on visual-verbal paired associate learning demonstrated in Chapter 6, provide a possible resolution of this paradox, because this situation is demonstrably similar to the early stages of learning to read.   Even in this case, however, a possible explanation of the results could be in terms of the improved visual recognition of the stimuli following tracing.   Other observations suggested that tracing does have effects on the verbal component of this task.   If this were substantiated it would provide a coherent explanation for any beneficial effects of tracing in remedial teaching which was also consistent with evidence about the retarded readers' cognitive impairments.   These theoretical questions will be expanded upon in the next section.

This leads naturally to a consideration of the further research needed to improve our understanding of how tracing may help in teaching retarded readers.   The questions here seem to centre on the effects of tracing on visual-verbal paired associate learning.   A good starting point would be to repeat Experiment 14 with matched groups of normal and retarded readers.   This would provide further evidence relevant to the verbal paired associate learning deficit often reported for these children (p. 52).   It would also be of interest to see whether tracing in this situation led to a greater improvement in performance amongst the retarded than the normal readers. This might be expected on the basis of the retarded readers being particularly poor on such tasks. An additional question which could be addressed in a study of this kind is the mechanism responsible for the improvement in paired associate learning produced by tracing. In particular, systematic evidence could be obtained as to whether verbal responses paired with forms which had been traced around occurred as intrusive responses to forms which had not been traced. If this observation, which was made while conducting Experiment 14, were substantiated it would be evidence in favour of the view that tracing in this situation has effects on the verbal component of the task. As noted above this would in turn provide a rationale for why tracing might be of special help to retarded readers when learning to read.

Another more general question raised by this research is whether writing movements may be important in the development of reading and spelling skills in normal children. One intuitively appealing idea is that even for children of normal ability, writing movements may provide an additional source of information which helps in learning spelling patterns. It seems likely that spelling, especially in the case of phonetically irregular words, depends upon visual memory for the appearance of words. Given the evidence presented here, that tracing around forms improves visual recognition, writing movements may well play a similar role in the learning of spelling patterns.

There does not appear to be any good evidence in favour of this view. It is interesting, however, that people sometimes report that writing out possible variants of a word helps them to decide on the correct spelling pattern. This is certainly consistent with the idea that writing movements are involved in memorising spelling patterns. The reliability of these subjective reports could be tested experimentally. For example, one could have subjects judge the acceptability of spelling patterns, with or without the opportunity to write them. Given the view advanced here subjects should be better at this task when they are allowed to write the words. In this experimental situation it would be necessary to prevent subjects from seeing the results of writing the words. If this were not done it would be possible to attribute any improvement following writing to the subjects being able to see the word in the familiar form of their own handwriting.

This hypothesis is also relevant to considering children with spelling problems. One promising line of research in this area concerns the problems of 'clumsy' children. This is a heterogeneous group of children with minor or uncertain neurological impairments, who are characterised by their marked difficulties of movement. It has been claimed that these children also often experience difficulties in learning to spell which are out of line with their age and IQ (Gubbay, 1975). The present line of reasoning suggests that the spelling problems of some of these children may be caused by their failure to learn the motor patterns associated with writing. In order to test this it would be interesting to apply the experimental techniques developed here. One could compare memory for series of forms when they are looked at, or looked at and traced around in clumsy children with and without spelling problems. If the above explanation is true, it would be predicted that while the good spellers would remember the forms better when they had traced around them, the poor spellers' memory for the forms would not be improved by the tracing.

## A POSSIBLE THEORETICAL SYNTHESIS

It seems appropriate at this stage to attempt a theoretical integration of the work in this book. Two major questions arise. First, it has been argued that a likely cause for most cases of reading retardation is some form of verbal memory deficit. Here detailed consideration will be given to the question of how verbal memory problems might lead to problems in learning to read. The second issue concerns how tracing around words may help retarded readers learn to read them, and how this may relate to their verbal memory problems. An attempt will be made to relate both these issues to current models of reading which have been developed in studies of adult fluent readers.

How might verbal memory problems cause problems in learning to read? It was argued in Chapter 6 that learning to read almost certainly involves visual-verbal paired associate learning. It seems likely that in the early stages of learning to read and perhaps especially for retarded readers (for reasons outlined in Chapter 6) a considerable number of words might be learned by rote, by simply learning an arbitrary association between certain spoken words and their written counterparts. The verbal memory difficulties of retarded readers would create problems at this most elementary stage of learning to read.

It is clear, however, that learning to read involves much more than the simple rote learning of arbitrary associations between the spoken and written forms of words. In view of the number of words which literate adults can read, complete reliance on such a strategy would be grossly inefficient (Savin, 1972). Equally, it is obvious that normal children and adults bring another strategy to bear in reading which is a generative one based on the phonological rules of our alphabetic writing system. Because the sounds in spoken language are represented in an orderly, if complex, way by letters of the alphabet, it becomes possible to generate the sound of a novel word from its written form. People's ability to do this is demonstrated by their ability to pronounce non-words which comply to the rules of English spelling patterns. So, for example, most people would pronounce the non-word 'brane' in the same way as the English word 'brain'.

It seems that the verbal memory problems of retarded readers would also hamper the acquisition of such phonological skills. In the first place, their verbal memory problems will cause difficulties in simply learning the names and sounds of the letters of the alphabet. Several of the retarded readers seen in Experiment 1 were slow to name letters, and some were uncertain and made errors in naming letters. This type of difficulty will obviously hinder the development of a phonological reading strategy, and as discussed in the Introduction to Chapter 6, there is certainly evidence that these children are impaired in their phonological reading skills. Such an impairment is likely to cause problems in learning to read because the child will be unable to decode novel words and so be unable to learn to read them without direct instruction.

There are other ways in which verbal memory problems might impede the development of phonological reading skills. As documented earlier (pp. 50-2) retarded readers have naming difficulties which appear to reflect a deficit in the retrieval of names from long term verbal memory. It could be argued that a child who finds it hard to produce a word and retain it will have great difficulty with the phonemic segmentation of words such as is involved in learning the correspondence between speech sounds and the letters in words. It must be hard to analyse and take apart a word which itself is elusive. Conversely, the short term verbal memory problems of retarded readers may lead to difficulties with phonic blending.  Even if a written word were successfully decoded into a series of sounds, there may be difficulties in retaining such a sequence of sounds in order to blend them and so arrive at the correct pronunciation of the word.

For all these reasons the verbal memory problems of retarded readers are likely to lead to problems in learning to read.  In particular, it appears likely that the verbal memory problems of these children will make it difficult for them to translate written words into a spoken form.  This idea leads us to consider whether reading necessarily involves a phase in which the printed word is translated into a speech-like representation.  In order to do this we must turn to models developed in the study of fluent adult readers.

Reading might be defined as the process whereby meaning is extracted from written language.  Given this definition a major question for studies of reading is to specify the type of information a reader extracts from a printed word which enables him to understand its meaning.  Current models propose that every reader has acquired a store of information about the words of his language in a sort of internal dictionary or lexicon.  In this lexicon each word has a separate entry in which is stored information about the word's meaning, spelling and pronunciation.  It is then reasonable to ask how a reader seeing a printed word gains access to the information about its meaning stored in the lexicon (e.g. Barron, 1978; Coltheart, 1978; Coltheart, Davelaar, Jonasson and Besner, 1977).

Two broad and opposing views on this question have been proposed.  One class of model proposes that the reader must first translate the printed word into a speech-like (phonological) code.  This phonological code is then used to access the lexical entry containing the information specifying the word's meaning (e.g. Gough, 1972).  Such a view has parsimony; once the word has been translated into a phonological form reading then utilises the same mechanisms involved in understanding speech.  An opposing view is that phonological coding is unnecessary and that lexical access can occur directly from a visual representation of the word (e.g. Bower, 1970; Baron, 1973).

Many studies have attempted to provide experimental support for one or other of these opposing positions.  It is not proposed here to review all the studies to date.  Instead a few of the major experimental findings will be described. These suggest that in skilled readers both phonological and visual access to the lexicon may occur.

There is certainly ample evidence for phonological coding occurring during reading. For example, Corcoran (1966) found that when subjects were merely required to cancel the letter 'e' in a prose passage, more omission errors occurred in words in which the 'e' was silent than in words in which 'e' was pronounced. Thus, even in a task which presumably could be performed by a purely visual strategy subjects appear to recode what they read into a speech-like form. The question is whether such speech coding is functionally involved in reading.

Electromyographic recordings also indicate the presence of articulatory speech movements during reading. Hardyck and Petrinovitch (1970) used this technique to study the functional role of subvocal activity in reading. Their undergraduate subjects could suppress subvocal activity during easy reading without loss of comprehension. When reading difficult passages they found it harder to suppress their subvocalisations and attempts to do so led to poorer comprehension. In this experiment comprehension was measured by a memory test given after the passage had been read; it could be that the subvocal speech was needed to aid memory for the passage rather than to access the meanings of the individual words.

Evidence which favours such an interpretation comes from a study by Kleiman (1975) where it was attempted to impair speech recoding during reading by having subjects shadow auditorily presented digits. Shadowing had little effect on the decision times for visual and semantic judgments on single word pairs, but phonemic and sentence acceptability judgments were slowed down by shadowing. From this it was concluded that while the meaning of individual words can be accessed without speech coding (as in judging whether pairs of words had the same meaning) such recoding acts as a useful memory storage code to hold the wording of a sentence until semantic integration occurs.

A similar picture also emerges from some experiments by Levy (1975, 1977) in which subjects read, or listened to, sentences and prose passages. On some trials they had to count repeatedly from 1 to 10 to suppress speech recoding. Subjects' memory for the material was tested by requiring them to judge whether test sentences had occurred in what had been read. Changes were made to either the meaning or the wording of different test sentences. The counting impaired memory for both types of information in sentences that had been read, but not in sentences which had been

listened to.   Once again these experiments suggest that
memory for what has been read depends upon a speech based
memory code.

Another approach to the possible role of phonological
coding in reading has utilised lexical decision tasks.   In
these experiments subjects merely have to respond as
quickly as possible to indicate whether or not a given letter
string is an English word.   If all the non-words presented
are well formed in the sense of only containing letter
sequences which are possibilities according to the rules of
English orthography, it is reasonable to assume that subjects can only decide whether a given letter string is, or is
not, a word by consultating their lexicon.   These tasks are
therefore relevant to how lexical access is achieved.

The role of phonological encoding in lexical decision tasks
was first studied by Rubenstein, Lewis and Rubenstein
(1971).   The main effect which they considered supported
the view that phonological coding was occurring prior to
lexical access was that pseudohomophones (e.g. burd) produced slower 'No' responses than non-words (e.g. wesp).
This result has been replicated by others (Coltheart et al.,
1977;  Patterson and Marcel, 1977).   Furthermore, Patterson and Marcel found this effect to be absent in two phonemic
dyslexic patients, who were unable to pronounce such legal
non-words.   These patients appear to rely solely on the
visual appearance of words when reading.   This would lead
to the prediction that if the pseudohomophone effect were
based on visual similarity it would be magnified in these
patients.   The fact that it was absent is strong evidence
that the slower response times to pseudohomophones in lexical decision studies are due to phonological encoding rather
than to the fact that these letter strings are visually similar
to English words (Coltheart, 1978).

In a further experiment Coltheart, Jonasson, Davelaar
and Besner (quoted by Coltheart, 1978) investigated the
effects of the regularity of spelling patterns on lexical decision times.   The rationale for this derived from the argument that phonological encoding prior to lexical access can
only occur for words which comply to the rules of English
orthography (regular words).   Thus, if lexical access via
phonological encoding occurs in the lexical decision task
this should make 'Yes' responses to regular words faster
than to irregular words for which it is believed a phonological representation cannot be generated prior to lexical
access.   No difference in the speed of 'Yes' responses to

regular and irregular words was found, however. It was suggested that in normal circumstances verification that a word is a word may be done on a visual basis, without recourse to phonological encoding; i.e., that visual access to the lexicon is completed before phonological encoding is complete. Thus, in lexical decision experiments although words are being encoded phonologically, it appears that for real words subjects generally complete lexical access on the basis of visual information before phonological encoding has occurred. It must be noted, however, that there is no requirement in these experiments for the subject to gain access to the meaning of a word. So although these experiments show that a word/non-word decision is often made on the basis of visual information alone, this does not mean that access to the meaning of a word is normally achieved in this way.

An experiment by Baron (1973) can be interpreted as evidence that visual and phonological information may both be involved in reading for meaning. In one experiment subjects had to classify phrases on the basis of whether they made sense or not. There were three types of phrase here; those which made sense (e.g. He sees poorly; Nut and bolt), those which did not make sense, but which sounded sensible (e.g. He seas poorly), and those which did not make sense and neither looked nor sounded sensible (e.g. Nut and bout). If subjects habitually use a phonological route to word meanings in reading, in this situation they should be slower to reject nonsense phrases that sound sensible (e.g. He seas poorly), than those that do not (e.g. Nut and bout). Although subjects did not in fact take longer to reject such phrases (e.g. He seas poorly), they did make more errors on them, suggesting that phonological access to meaning was occurring. In a second experiment the same types of phrases were used, but in this case subjects were instructed to respond 'Yes' if the phrase sounded as though it made sense. In this case subjects took longer and made more errors in responding 'Yes' to phrases which sounded sensible, but looked wrong (e.g. He seas poorly), than to those which sounded and looked sensible (e.g. He sees poorly). This again suggests that subjects use both visual and phonological access to meaning; performance was fastest when these two forms of information were congruent, but when there was a conflict of information from these two sources performance was slower and less accurate.

These examples will suffice to show that there is considerable evidence for both visual and phonological access to the meaning of printed words by skilled readers. This conclusion appears to be widely accepted by workers in this field (e.g. Baron, 1977; Coltheart, 1978). The major questions now appear to concern the relative contributions of these different processes to reading in different situations and the extent to which these processes can be controlled by the subject.

One might object that these conclusions and the studies they are based upon are only relevant to adults' and not to children's reading. Only one published study has addressed the question of how children access the meaning of printed words, and this indicates that essentially the same dual coding mechanisms appear to be operative. Barron and Baron (1977) tested the plausible idea that in children just learning to read the indirect or phonological route to the meaning of words might predominate, with the visual route only becoming predominant after much practice. Children from $6\frac{1}{2}$ to $13\frac{1}{2}$ years old were shown picture-word pairs and asked to say whether the pairs rhymed in a sound task, or went together (were semantically related) in a meaning task. On half the trials in each condition the children were required to repeat the words 'double, double' out loud while making their judgments in an attempt to suppress phonological coding. In so far as the younger children relied more upon a phonological route for accessing the meaning of words, and on the (untested) assumption that repeating 'double, double' will impair the operation of this route, it was expected that the vocal interference should influence both their rhyme and meaning judgments but that it would have relatively less effect on the meaning judgments in the older children. Surprisingly, while the vocal interference task disrupted the rhyme judgments at all age levels it left the meaning task unimpaired in terms of both time and error scores at all age levels. Barron and Baron conclude that their results are consistent with studies of adults in indicating that the primary route from print to meaning when reading single words is a direct visual one. On the other hand, when the unrelated picture-word pairs in the meaning task had names which rhymed, the times and error rates in the meaning task increased. This suggested a subsidiary role for an indirect phonological route to meaning.

From this study it certainly appears that the same visual and phonological routes from print to meaning are operative when children read single words as when adults do so.

Differences in the use of these routes may of course exist which, for one reason or another, were not detected by the study. At the moment, however, it seems reasonable to accept the conclusion that qualitative differences in the use of these routes for accessing the meaning of individual printed words do not exist between adults and children. This in turn provides some justification for trying to draw together the research on reading in adults with that on children who experience reading problems.

Consideration of current models of reading which postulate a system of dual access to meaning via phonological and visual routes, raises interesting possibilities in relation to reading retardation. According to the arguments presented above, retarded readers may have particular difficulty generating a phonological representation of printed words. This difficulty is also present in brain damaged adults suffering from phonemic dyslexia. Further, as noted in Chapter 6, both these groups appear to make semantic errors when reading and find words of high imagery value much easier to read than those of low imagery value. The pattern of difficulties in phonemic dyslexia have been interpreted as suggesting they rely on the direct visual route from print to meaning when reading. According to this view, because they are unable to generate a phonological representation of a word prior to lexical access, they must rely on a direct visual route from print to meaning. Their success in pronouncing words they read presumably results from a look-up of information concerning the sound of the word stored in the lexicon, or at least must depend upon the results of lexical access. One possibility being that they go from the meaning of a word to its sound.

Given the similarities between reading retarded children and phonemic dyslexics an interesting hypothesis is that retarded readers may be reading by a visual route, or at least relying more upon such a route than normal readers as the phonemic dyslexics are hypothesised to do. An impairment in accessing the lexicon via a phonological route may provide an explanation for the retarded readers' problems. There are differences of opinion as to the extent to which the understanding of single words depends upon phonological access to the lexicon. Some argue for the likely involvement of phonological coding in understanding single words (e.g. Baron, 1977) while others argue that it may only be necessary to concede a role to phonological coding when understanding depends upon extensive memory requirements (e.g. Barron, 1978).  It is clear that the reading problems of retarded readers are just as evident in the reading of single words as in the reading of prose.  If phonological encoding difficulties are to explain their reading problems they must be related to the processes operating in the reading of single words.  Some experiments dealing with the reading of numbers do suggest a role for phonological coding in understanding single words.  These will be briefly described, because they support the idea that an impairment in phonological coding may lead to difficulties in understanding single words.  They also provide a possible means for evaluating the hypothesis that retarded readers suffer from such an impairment.

Numbers provide interesting possibilities for work on reading because they have alternative representations as either words or numerals.  Numbers written alphabetically (one, two, etc.) are associated with their spoken names by means of phonological rules.  Numerals on the other hand must be associated with their names on a purely arbitrary basis.  Recent experiments suggest these differences have psychological implications for the way in which they are read by skilled readers.

Baron (1977) presented subjects with lists of either the Roman numbers 'I' to 'IV' or the words 'one' to 'four'. There were two tasks.  In one task the subject had to check off each item which was larger than the one that had preceded it.  In the other the subject had to add one to the number represented by each item and write the answer as an Arabic numeral.  On half the trials in each task subjects had to count backwards from 10 to 1 to impair phonological encoding.

The hypothesis suggested by Baron was that for numbers represented as words two routes to meaning are available; direct visual access to the meaning and indirect access via the pronunciation derived from the spelling pattern of the word.  For the Roman numerals, however, only visual access to meaning is possible because the numerals contain no information about their pronunciation.  This leads to the idea that access to the meaning of the numbers represented as words may depend upon both the direct visual and indirect phonological routes.  For the Roman numerals, however, only the direct visual route will be available.  From this it was predicted that the vocal interference task should have more effect on understanding numbers presented as words than those presented as Roman numerals.  This prediction was confirmed; vocal interference had more effect on both tasks when the numbers were presented in word form.

The conclusion that readers extract the meaning from Roman numerals and alphabetical representations of numbers differently seems inescapable from this experiment. The most natural explanation as Baron points out is that access to the meaning of alphabetically represented numbers is partially dependent upon a phonological stage. In this situation the phonological code appears to play a role in the extraction of meaning even from single words; when this mechanism was impaired by vocal interference performance was slowed down.

A quite separate experiment reaches the same conclusion about the psychological importance of the differences between alphabetic and numeral representations of numbers. Besner and Coltheart (1979) measured the times taken to decide which of a pair of numbers was numerically larger. In the first experiment the pairs of numbers were presented as Arabic numerals (1, 2, etc.). The physical size of the numerals was also varied. On some trials the numerically larger numeral was also physically larger, on some trials the two numerals were the same size; on the remaining trials the numerically larger numeral was physically smaller. This gives three conditions referred to as 'Congruent', 'Same size' and 'Incongruent' respectively.

The results showed that subjects' decisions were fastest in the Congruent condition, slowest in the Incongruent condition, and intermediate in the Same Size condition. Irrelevant variations in the physical size of the numerals affected the time taken to decide on their relative magnitude.

In a second experiment, the procedure was essentially identical except that there were only two conditions (Congruent v Incongruent) and the numbers were represented alphabetically (one, two, etc.). Here irrelevant variations in physical size had no effect whatever on the time taken to decide which of the two numbers was numerically larger.

These results were related to a finding of Paivio (1975) who gave subjects the task of deciding which of two simultaneously presented animals was the larger in real life. The animals were represented as pictures or words and the physical sizes of the words or pictures varied so that the physical size relationship was sometimes congruent and sometimes incongruent with the relationship of the real life sizes. Congruence facilitated, and incongruence impaired judgments with pictures, but there was no effect of congruence or incongruence when the stimuli were words.

The fact that such similar effects occur with Arabic numerals and pictures was taken to suggest that these different stimuli are processed by skilled readers in a similar way. This can be related to Baron's experiment described above. While numerals have a direct, visual access to meaning (which is not impaired by vocal interference but is affected by irrelevant variations in the physical size of stimuli) alphabetically presented numbers gain access to meaning at least partially via a phonological route (because of this vocal interference impairs access to their meaning but irrelevant variations in physical size do not affect this process).

Given the assumption (which in the absence of any counter evidence seems reasonable) that understanding the meaning of written numbers is comparable to understanding the meaning of other written words, these experiments provide interesting evidence relevant to the processes occurring during reading. The results suggest that phonological processing is involved in reading the meaning of single words, where memory requirements are minimal. The techniques used in these experiments also appear to provide possible ways of testing the hypothesis advanced here that retarded readers rely more upon the direct visual route, than the indirect phonological route, than do normal children when reading.

One possible test of this hypothesis would be to compare the performance of normal and retarded readers on the experimental task used by Baron (1977) described above. Baron found that vocal interference impaired reading the meaning of numbers represented alphabetically much more than of those represented by Roman numerals. This was taken as evidence for phonological processing being involved in reading the meaning of alphabetically written numbers but not the Roman numerals. If retarded readers rely less upon a phonological strategy and more upon a visual strategy in reading than do normal readers, the effects of vocal interference on these two tasks should vary between the two groups. When reading numerals it is thought that only a direct visual route to meaning is used. If this is the case, and given that this route is equally efficient in both retarded and normal readers, performance with these stimuli should not differ between the groups, and counting should have an equal effect upon performance in both groups. When reading alphabetically presented numbers a phonological strategy is thought to play a role. If such phonological encoding is impaired in retarded readers, when reading alphabetic numbers we might expect them to perform more poorly than the normal readers and more critically, vocal interference might be expected to have less effect upon their performance than in the case of normal readers. Such an experiment would appear to be simple enough to carry out with children, and would provide evidence relevant to the ideas presented here.

These ideas about the codes employed in lexical access by retarded readers may also be related, if tenuously, to the mechanisms underlying any possible effects of tracing in remedial teaching. The two possible effects of tracing on the process of learning to read which were discussed in Chapter 6 can be phrased in terms of the codes used for lexical access.

First, if retarded readers do rely more upon a direct visual route to meaning, tracing might enhance this because of its effect on visual recognition. Experiments in earlier chapters have shown that tracing forms improves subsequent visual recognition of them. Tracing words might reasonably be expected to improve visual memory for them and this in turn might improve the learning of direct links between a word's appearance and its meaning.

A second possibility, also discussed in Chapter 6, is that tracing may improve the use of phonological encoding by retarded readers. Specifically, in Experiment 14, tracing was shown to improve visual-verbal paired associate learning - names paired with forms were learned more quickly when the forms were traced around. Similarly, tracing words may help the retarded reader learn to associate their written and spoken forms. Such learning will then make an indirect phonological route to word meanings available.

In summary, the arguments presented here indicate that the demonstrated verbal memory problems of retarded readers provide a likely explanation for these children's difficulties in learning to read. Some of the possible links between verbal memory problems and difficulties in learning to read have been outlined. In addition, consideration of current models of reading, and of the pattern of deficits shown by phonemic dyslexic patients and retarded readers, lead to the idea that the level of reading achieved by retarded readers may depend in part upon different mechanisms to the reading of normal children. In particular it seems plausible that these children place less reliance on a phonological code when reading than do normal children. These

ideas remain highly speculative, but they provide a unifying
framework which relates the observed cognitive deficits of
retarded readers to their reading problems, and also relates
these problems to the possible mechanisms whereby tracing
may help them learn to read. An experiment was suggested
that would provide evidence relevant to these ideas.

Two broader points also emerge from this discussion.
First, the similarities between children retarded in reading
and adult phonemic dyslexic patients have been mentioned.
The similarities between these two groups which have been
revealed so far suggest that it would be fruitful to look for
further similarities. Comparisons of this sort obviously
present complex problems. In the one case we are dealing
with a failure of reading skills to develop normally while in
the other we are looking at the breakdown of an acquired
and practised skill. In view of this, even if these groups
share some common underlying deficit, its manifestations
may vary. Strategies may be available to the phonemic dyslexic patient to circumvent his difficulties which are not open
to a child who has never mastered the skill of reading. In
the light of this the similarities which have been reported to
date between these two groups are very encouraging.

A second general point which follows from the present discussion is that it would seem advisable to try and apply the
sorts of techniques used in studying reading in adults to the
study of retarded readers. This would facilitate the forma-
tion of links between current models of reading and explanations of the difficulties experienced by retarded readers.
This would be likely to be of benefit to both fields. On the
one hand it should improve our understanding of reading
retardation, by providing new techniques to apply to the
study of these children, and new theories to provide a conceptual framework for experimental findings. Conversely,
such research may increase our understanding of normal
reading processes. For example, if it could be shown that
retarded readers were impaired in the use of phonological
codes for lexical access, this would provide further evidence
for the functional role of such codes in reading and in learning to read.

## THE RELATIONSHIP BETWEEN PSYCHOLOGY AND EDUCATION

It is hoped that the present work represents an example of the fruitful, if limited, interplay between psychology and education. The approach adopted here is straightforward: if a certain educational procedure is reputed to be effective it seems reasonable to explore the procedure experimentally to gain evidence as to its effectiveness, and the mechanisms responsible for this. Such interplay ought to be of benefit to both disciplines. In the present case, it is hoped that the experiments reported here put the use of tracing as a teaching aid on a firmer footing.

Conversely, the experiments have also added something to psychological knowledge. The fact that tracing improves visual recognition certainly could not have been predicted on the basis of previous work. Indeed, this finding ran counter to the author's initial prejudices. This of course is precisely the value of experiments; they allow us to test ideas in a way in which a priori argument and debate cannot.

In addition to this the experiments in Chapter 4 tell us something about the storage and integration of information from different sensory modalities. The differential effects of motor and visual interference on memory for forms visually inspected or visually inspected and traced around, demonstrates both that visual and motor information are stored in separate short term storage systems, and also that at some level of abstraction this information is represented in some common code.

As well as these positive contributions, the present work also focuses on the limitations of knowledge in certain areas. One example of this may be taken from Chapter 5, where some inadequacies in our knowledge of visual memory processes were apparent. Another aspect of this same point was made earlier in this chapter, where our ignorance concerning the effects of visual similarity on memory were noted.

The present work, then, is an example of an interaction between psychology and education in which a method of educational practice has been explored by employing the methods and theories developed by experimental psychologists. An alternative approach would be to apply ideas current in psychology to education. Given our present level of knowledge in psychology, the value of formulating general prescriptions for educational practice would appear dubious. Few, if any, of the findings of experimental psychology appear solid or well understood enough to justify this. Also, even given well established knowledge about certain psychological processes, the educational implications of such knowledge are often not clear. For example, even if it could be established that before a certain age children were unable to perform transitive inferences (cf. Bryant, 1974; Bryant and Kopytynska, 1976), what would follow? One might argue that any skills which required such logical operations should not be taught to children below this age. An alternative, however, would be to train such tasks in order to bring on the acquisition of such a basic and important logical skill.

This is not to argue that psychologists should never attempt to prescribe procedures to be applied to education. It does appear, however, that two caveats are relevant to such attempts. First, that such recommendations ought to be tied closely to the sorts of situations which have been directly studied. Second, it seems of paramount importance that such recommendations should be carefully evaluated by research into their effectiveness. If these factors are borne in mind, it seems reasonable to hope that psychology might have a considerable and beneficial effect upon educational practice. It might help to clarify these issues by returning to an example concerning reading retardation.

From the research reviewed in Chapter 1, it seems likely that many retarded readers experience difficulties in segmenting spoken words into their constituent phonemes, and also in appreciating the similarities in sound between words. Such difficulties would appear likely to contribute to their difficulties in learning to read. Given this, a reasonable teaching strategy would be to attempt to train such skills in these children, in the hope that this training would help to alleviate their reading problems. It would appear important, however, to evaluate the effectiveness of such procedures in a controlled study before they were applied generally to teaching these children.

# References

ALEXANDER, D. and MONEY, J. (1965). Reading ability, object constancy, and Turner's syndrome, 'Perceptual and Motor Skills', 20, 981-4.

AUDLEY, R.J. (1976). Reading difficulties: the importance of basic research in solving practical problems, Presidential address, British Association for the Advancement of Science, Section J.

AVERBACH, E. and CORIELL, A.S. (1961). Short-term memory in vision, 'Bell System Technical Journal', 40, 309-28.

BAKKER, D.J. (1967). Temporal order, meaningfulness and reading ability, 'Perceptual and Motor Skills', 24, 1027-30.

BAKKER, D.J. (1972). 'Temporal Order in Disturbed Reading', Rotterdam University Press.

BAKWIN, H. (1973). Reading disability in twins, 'Developmental Medicine and Child Neurology', 15, 184-7.

BARON, J. (1973). Phonemic stage not necessary for reading, 'Quarterly Journal of Experimental Psychology', 25, 241-6.

BARON, J. (1977). Mechanisms for pronouncing printed words: use and acquisition, in D. LaBerge and S.J. Samuels (eds), 'Basic Processes in Reading: Perception and Comprehension', Erlbaum, Hillsdale, New Jersey.

BARRON, R.W. (1978). Access to the meanings of printed words: some implications for reading and learning to read, in F.B. Murray (ed.), 'The Development of the Reading Process', International Reading Association Monograph (no. 3), International Reading Association, Newark.

BARRON, R.W. and BARON, J. (1977). How children get meaning from printed words, 'Child Development', 48, 587-94.

177

BEERY, J.W. (1967). Matching of auditory and visual stimuli by average and retarded readers, 'Child Development', 38, 827-33.

BELMONT, L. and BIRCH, H.G. (1966). The intellectual profile of retarded readers, 'Perceptual and Motor Skills', 22, 787-816.

BENTON, A.L. (1962). Dyslexia in relation to form perception and directional sense, in J. Money (ed.), 'Reading Disability: Progress and Research Needs in Dyslexia', Johns Hopkins Press, Baltimore.

BERGER, M., YULE, W. and RUTTER, M. (1975). Attainment and adjustment in two geographical areas, II: The prevalence of specific reading retardation, 'British Journal of Psychiatry', 126, 510-19.

BERMAN, A. (1939). The influence of the kinaesthetic factor in the perception of symbols in partial reading disability, 'Journal of Educational Psychology', 30, 187-98.

BESNER, D. and COLTHEART, M. (1979). Ideographic and alphabetic processing in skilled reading of English, 'Neuropsychologia', 17, 467-72.

BIRCH, H.G. and BELMONT, L. (1964). Auditory-visual integration in normal and retarded readers, 'American Journal of Orthopsychiatry', 34, 852-61.

BLANK, M. (1968). Cognitive processes in auditory discrimination in normal and retarded readers, 'Child Development', 39, 1091-101.

BLANK, M. and BRIDGER, W.H. (1966). Deficiencies in verbal labelling in retarded readers, 'American Journal of Orthopsychiatry', 36, 840-7.

BLANK, M., WEIDER, S. and BRIDGER, W.H. (1968). Verbal deficiencies in abstract thinking in early reading retardation, 'American Journal of Orthopsychiatry', 38, 823-34.

BODER, E.M. (1973). Developmental dyslexia: a diagnostic approach based on three atypical reading-spelling patterns, 'Developmental Medicine and Child Neurology', 15, 663-87.

BOWER, T.G.R. (1970), Reading by eye, in H. Levin and J.P. Williams (eds), 'Basic Studies in Reading', Basic Books, New York.

BRADLEY, L. and BRYANT, P.E. (1978). Difficulties in auditory organisation as a possible cause of reading backwardness, 'Nature', 271, 746-7.

BRADLEY, L. and BRYANT, P.E. (1979). The independence of reading and spelling in backward and normal readers, 'Developmental Medicine and Child Neurology', 21, 504-14.

BRADLEY, L., HULME C. and BRYANT, P.E. (1979). The connexion between different verbal difficulties in a backward reader: a case study, 'Developmental Medicine and Child Neurology', 21, 790-5.

BRYANT, P.E. (1974). 'Perception and Understanding in Young Children', Methuen, London.

BRYANT, P.E. (1975). Cross modal development and reading, in D.D. Duane and M.B. Rawson (eds), 'Reading, Perception and Language', York Press, Baltimore.

BRYANT, P.E. and BRADLEY, L. (1980). Why children sometimes write words which they do not read, in U. Frith (ed.), 'Cognitive Processes in Spelling', Academic Press, London.

BRYANT, P.E. and KOPYTYNSKA, H. (1976). Spontaneous measurement by young children, 'Nature', 260, 773.

BRYDEN, M.P. (1972). Auditory-visual and sequential matching in relation to reading ability, 'Child Development', 43, 824-32.

BULLOCK, A. (1975). 'A Language for Life', HMSO, London.

CARROLL, H.C.M. (1972). The remedial teaching of reading: an evaluation, 'Remedial Education', 7, 10-15.

CASHDAN, S. and ZUNG, B.J. (1970). Effect of sensory modality and delay on form recognition, 'Journal of Experimental Psychology', 86, 458-60.

CIPOLLA, C.M. (1969). 'Literacy and Development in the West', Penguin Books, Harmondsworth.

CLARK, M.M. (1970), 'Reading Difficulties in Schools', Penguin Books, Harmondsworth.

CLIFTON-EVEREST, I.M. (1976). Dyslexia: is there a disorder of visual perception?, 'Neuropsychologia', 14, 491-4.

COLTHEART, M. (1978). Lexical access in simple reading tasks, in G. Underwood (ed.), 'Strategies of Information Processing', Academic Press, London.

COLTHEART, M., DAVELAAR, E., JONASSON, J. and BESNER, D. (1977). Access to the internal lexicon, in S. Dornic (ed.), 'Attention and Performance VI', Academic Press, London.

CONNOLLY, K. and JONES, B. (1970). A developmental study of afferent-reafferent integration, 'British Journal of Psychology', 61, 259-66.

CONRAD, R. (1964). Acoustic confusions in immediate memory, 'British Journal of Psychology', 55, 75-84.

CONRAD, R. (1971). The chronology of the development of covert speech in children, 'Developmental Psychology', 5, 398–405.

CONRAD, R. (1977). The reading ability of deaf school leavers, 'British Journal of Educational Psychology', 47, 138–48.

CONRAD, R. (1979). 'The Deaf School Child: Language and Cognitive Function', Harper & Row, London.

CONRAD, R. and HULL, A.J. (1964). Information, acoustic confusion and memory span, 'British Journal of Psychology', 55, 429–32.

CORCORAN, D.W.J. (1974). An acoustic factor in letter cancellation, 'Nature', 210, 658.

CORKIN, S. (1974). Serial ordering deficits in inferior readers, 'Neuropsychologia', 12, 347–54.

COTTERELL, G.C. (1970a). Teaching procedures, in A.W. Franklin and S. Naidoo (eds), 'Assessment and Teaching of Dyslexic Children', Invalid Children's Aid Association, London.

COTTERELL, G.C. (1970b). The Fernald auditory-kinaesthetic technique, in A.W. Franklin and S. Naidoo (eds), 'Assessment and Teaching of Dyslexic Children', Invalid Children's Aid Association, London.

CRITCHLEY, M. (1970). 'The Dyslexic Child', Heinemann, London.

DAVIE, R., BUTLER, N.R. and GOLDSTEIN, H. (1972). 'From Birth to Seven', Longmans, London.

DE HIRSCH, K., JANSKY, J.J. and LANGFORD, W.S. (1966). 'Predicting Reading Failure', Harper & Row, New York.

DENCKLA, M.B. and RUDEL, R.G. (1976). Rapid automatised naming: dyslexia differentiated from other learning disabilities, 'Neuropsychologia', 14, 471–9.

DENNER, B. and CASHDAN, S. (1967). Sensory processing and the recognition of forms in nursery-school children, 'British Journal of Psychology', 38, 101–4.

DEUTSCH, C.P. (1964). Auditory discrimination and learning: social factors, 'Merrill Palmer Quarterly', 10, 277–96.

DIEWERT, G.L. (1975). Retention and coding in motor short term memory: a comparison of storage codes for distance and location information, 'Journal of Motor Behaviour', 7, 183–90.

DOEHRING, D.G. (1968). 'Patterns of Impairment in Specific Reading Disability', Indiana University Press, Bloomington.

DOEHRING, D.G. and HOSHKO, I.M. (1977). Classification of reading problems by the Q-technique of factor analysis, 'Cortex', 13, 281-94.

DOUGLAS, J.W.B. (1964). 'The Home and the School'. MacGibbon & Kee, London.

DOUGLAS, J.W.B., ROSS, J.M. and SIMPSON, H.R. (1968). 'All our Future', Peter Davies, London.

DOWNING, J. (1973). 'Comparative Reading', Macmillan, New York.

ETAUGH, C.F. (1970). Factors in learning stereometric discriminations in children, 'Perceptual and Motor Skills', 30, 614.

FAUST-ADAMS, A.S. (1972). Interference in short-term retention of discrete movements, 'Journal of Experimental Psychology', 96, 400-6.

FERNALD, G.M. (1943). 'Remedial Techniques in Basic School Subjects', McGraw-Hill, New York.

FERNALD, G.M. and KELLER, H.B. (1921). The effect of kinaesthetic factors in the development of word recognition in the case of non-readers, 'Journal of Educational Research', 4, 355-77.

FICO, J.M. and BRODSKY, H.S. (1972). The effect of visual and tactual stimulation on learning of abstract forms, 'Psychonomic Science', 27, 246-8.

FISHER, J. (1905). Case of congenital word-blindness (inability to learn to read), 'Opthalmic Review', 24, 315-18.

FORSTER, M. (1941). Visual and visual-kinaesthetic learning in reading nonsense syllables, 'Journal of Educational Psychology', 32, 452-8.

FRANK. H. (1936). 'Word-blindness' in school children, 'Transactions of the Opthalmological Society of the U.K.', 56, 231-8.

GARFIELD, J.C. (1964). Motor impersistence in normal and brain damaged children, 'Neurology', 14, 623-30.

GASCON, G. and GOODGLASS, H. (1970). Reading retardation and the information content of stimuli in paired associate learning, 'Cortex', 6, 417-29.

GECHSWIND, N. (1965). Disconnexion syndromes in animals and man. Part I, 'Brain', 88, 237-94.

GIBSON, J.J. and GIBSON, E.J. (1955). Perceptual learning: differentiation or enrichment?, 'Psychological Review', 62, 33-40.

GIBSON, E.J., GIBSON, J.J., PICK, A.D. and OSSER, H. (1962). A developmental study of the discrimination of letter-like forms, 'Journal of Comparative and Physiological Psychology', 55, 897-906.

GIBSON, E.J. and LEVIN, H. (1975).  'The Psychology of Reading', MIT, Cambridge, Mass.

GILLINGHAM, A.M. and STILLMAN, B.U. (1956).  'Remedial Training for Children with Specific Disability in Reading, Spelling and Penmanship' (5th edition), Sackett & Wilhelms, New York.

GOLDSTEIN, K. (1948).  'Language and Language Disturbances'.  Grune & Stratton, New York.

GOUGH, P.B. (1972).  One second of reading, in J.F. Kavanagh and J.G. Mattingley (eds), 'Language by Ear and by Eye', MIT Press, Cambridge, Mass.

GOYEN, J.D. and LYLE, J.G. (1971a).  Effect of incentives and age on the visual recognition of retarded readers, 'Journal of Experimental Child Psychology', 11, 266-73.

GOYEN, J.D. and LYLE, J.G. (1971b).  Effect of incentives upon retarded and normal readers on a visual associate learning task, 'Journal of Experimental Child Psychology', 11, 274-80.

GOYEN, J.D. and LYLE, J.G. (1973).  STM and visual discrimination in retarded readers, 'Perceptual and Motor Skills', 36, 403-8.

GUBBAY, S. (1975).  'The Clumsy Child', Saunders, London.

GUMMERMAN, K. and GRAY, C.R. (1972).  Age, iconic storage and visual information processing, 'Journal of Experimental Child Psychology', 13, 165-70.

HAARHOOF, T. (1920).  'Schools of Gaul', Oxford University Press, London.

HALLGREN, B. (1950).  Specific dyslexia ('congenital word-blindness'): a clinical and genetic study, 'Acta Psychiatrica et Neurologica', Supplement, 65.

HARDYCK, C.D. and PETRINOVITCH, L.F. (1970).  Subvocal speech and comprehension level as a function of the difficulty level of reading materials, 'Journal of Verbal Learning and Verbal Behaviour', 9, 647-52.

HARRIS, G.J. and BURKE, D. (1972).  The effects of grouping on short-term serial recall of digits by children: developmental trends, 'Child Development', 43, 710-16.

HENRY, S. (1947).  Children's audiograms in relation to reading attainment, 'Journal of Genetic Psychology', 70, 211-31 and 71, 49-63.

HERMANN, K. (1959).  'Reading Disability: A Medical Study of Word-Blindness and Related Handicaps', Munksgaard, Copenhagen.

HINE, W.D. (1970).  The abilities of partially hearing

children, 'British Journal of Educational Psychology', 40, 171-8.

HINSHELWOOD, J. (1895). Word-blindness and visual memory, 'Lancet', 2, 1564-70.

HINSHELWOOD, J. (1900). 'Letter-, Word-, and Mind-Blindness', Lewis, London.

HINSHELWOOD, J. (1917). 'Congenital Word-Blindness', Lewis, London.

HOLMES, D.L. and PEPER, R.J. (1977). An evaluation of the use of spelling error analysis in the diagnosis of reading disabilities, 'Child Development', 48, 1708-11.

HUELSMAN, C.B. (1970). The WISC subtest syndrome for disabled readers, 'Perceptual and Motor Skills', 30, 535-50.

INGRAM, T.T.S. (1970). The nature of dyslexia, in F.A. Young and D.B. Lindsley (eds), 'Early Experience and Visual Information Processing in Perceptual and Reading Disorders', National Academy of Sciences, Washington, DC.

INGRAM, T.T.S. and REID, J.F. (1956). Developmental aphasia observed in a department of child psychiatry, 'Archives of Disabled Children', 31, 161-72.

JAMES, W. (1890). 'Principles of Psychology', vol. 2, Heinemann, London.

JENSEN, A.R. (1969). How much can we boost IQ and scholastic achievement?, 'Harvard Educational Review', 39, 1-123.

JENSEN, N.J. and KING, E.M. (1970). Effects of different kinds of visual motor training in learning to read words, 'Journal of Educational Psychology', 61, 90-6.

JORM, A.F. (1977). Effect of word imagery on reading performance as a function of reader ability, 'Journal of Educational Psychology', 69, 46-54.

KAMIN, L.J. (1974). 'The Science and Politics of IQ', Erlbaum, Potomac.

KANTOWITZ, B.H. (1972). Interference in short-term motor memory: interpolated task difficulty, similarity or activity?, 'Journal of Experimental Psychology', 95, 264-74.

KAWI, A.A. and PASAMANICK, B. (1958). Association of factors of pregnancy with reading disorders in childhood, 'Journal of the American Medical Association', 166, 1420-3.

KAWI, A.A. and PASAMANICK, B. (1959). Prenatal and paranatal factors in the development of childhood reading disorders, 'Monographs of the Society for Research in Child Development', 24, 4.

KELLICUT, M.H., PARKS, T.E., KROLL, N.E.A. and SALZBERG, P.M. (1973). Visual memory as indicated by the latency of recognition for normal and reversed letters, 'Journal of Experimental Psychology', 97, 387-90.

KINSBOURNE, M. and WARRINGTON, E.K. (1963). Developmental factors in reading and writing backwardness, 'British Journal of Psychology', 54, 145-56.

KIRK, S.A. (1933). The influence of manual tracing on the learning of simple words in the case of subnormal boys, 'Journal of Educational Psychology', 24, 525-35.

KIRK, S.A. and KIRK, W.D. (1971). 'Psycholinguistic Learning Disabilities, Diagnosis and Remediation', University of Illinois Press, Urbana.

KLEIMAN, G.M. (1975). Speech recoding in reading, 'Journal of Verbal Learning and Verbal Behaviour', 14, 323-39.

KROLL, N.E.A., PARKS, T., PARKINSON, S.R., BIEBER, S.L. and JOHNSON, A.L. (1970). Short-term memory while shadowing: recall of visually and aurally presented letters, 'Journal of Experimental Psychology', 85, 220-4.

LACHMANN, F.M. (1960), Perceptual-motor development in children retarded in reading ability, 'Journal of Consulting Psychology', 24, 427-31.

LESLIE, L. (1975). Susceptibility to interference effects in short term memory of normal and retarded readers, 'Perceptual and Motor Skills', 40, 791-4.

LEVIN, H., WATSON, J.S. and FELDMAN, M. (1964). Writing as pretraining for association learning, 'Journal of Educational Psychology', 55, 181-4.

LEVY, B.A. (1975). Vocalisation and suppression effects in sentence memory, 'Journal of Verbal Learning and Verbal Behaviour', 14, 304-16.

LEVY, B.A. (1977), Reading: speech and meaning processes, 'Journal of Verbal Learning and Verbal Behaviour', 16, 623-38.

LIBERMAN, I.Y. (1973). Segmentation of the spoken word and reading acquisition, 'Bulletin of the Orton Society', 23, 65-77.

LIBERMAN, I.Y., SHANKWEILER, D., FISCHER, F.W. and CARTER, B. (1974). Explicit syllable and phoneme segmentation in the young child, 'Journal of Experimental Child Psychology', 18, 201-12.

LIBERMAN, I.Y., SHANKWEILER, D., LIBERMAN, A.M., FOWLER, C. and FISCHER, F.W. (1977). Phonetic segmentation and recoding in the beginning reader, in A.S. Reber and D. Scarborough (eds), 'Toward a Psychology of Reading', Lawrence Erlbaum, Hillsdale, New Jersey.

LIBERMAN, I.Y., SHANKWEILER, D., ORLANDO, C., HARRIS, K.S. and BERTI, F.B. (1971). Letter confusions and reversals of sequence in the beginning reader: implications for Orton's theory of developmental dyslexia, 'Cortex', 7, 127-42.

LINGREN, R.H. (1969). Performance of disabled and normal readers on the Bender-Gestalt auditory discrimination test and visual motor matching, 'Perceptual and Motor Skills', 29, 152-4.

LYLE, J.G. (1968a). Performance of retarded readers on the memory-for-designs test, 'Perceptual and Motor Skills', 26, 851-4.

LYLE, J.G. (1968b). Errors of retarded readers on block designs, 'Perceptual and Motor Skills', 26, 1222.

LYLE, J.G. (1970). Certain ante-natal, perinatal and developmental variables and reading retardation in middle class boys, 'Child Development', 41, 481-91.

LYLE, J.G. and GOYEN, J.D. (1968). Visual recognition, developmental lag and strephosymbolia in reading retardation, 'Journal of Abnormal Psychology', 73, 25-9.

LYLE, J.G. and GOYEN, J.D. (1969). Performance of retarded readers on the WISC and educational tests, 'Journal of Abnormal Psychology', 74, 1-5-12.

LYLE, J.G. and GOYEN, J.D. (1975). Effect of speed of exposure and difficulty of discrimination on visual recognition of retarded readers, 'Journal of Abnormal Psychology', 84, 673-6.

MCLEOD, J. (1965). A comparison of WISC sub-test scores of pre-adolescent successful and unsuccessful readers, 'Australian Journal of Psychology', 17, 220-8.

MACCOBY, E.E. and JACKLIN, C.N. (1975). 'The Psychology of Sex Differences', Oxford University Press, London.

MACHOWSKY, H. and MEYERS, J. (1975). Auditory discrimination, intelligence and reading achievement at Grade 1, 'Perceptual and Motor Skills', 40, 363-8.

MARCEL, T. and PATTERSON, K. (1977). Word recognition and production: reciprocity in clinical and normal studies, in J. Requin (ed.), 'Attention and Performance VI', Erlbaum, Hillsdale, New Jersey.

MARK, L.S., SHANKWEILER, D., LIBERMAN, I.Y. and
FOWLER, C.A. (1977). Phonetic recoding and reading
difficulty in beginning readers, 'Memory and Cognition',
5, 623-9.

MARTIN, E. (1967). Stimulus recognition in aural paired
associate learning, 'Journal of Verbal Learning and
Verbal Behaviour', 6, 272-6.

MATTIS, S., FRENCH, J.H. and RAPIN, I. (1975).
Dyslexia in children and young adults: three independent
neuropsychological syndromes, 'Developmental Medicine
and Child Neurology', 17, 150-63.

MELTZOFF, A.N. and MOORE, M.K. (1977). Imitation of
facial and manual gestures by human neonates, 'Science',
198, 75-8.

MILLAR, S. (1971). Visual and haptic cue utilisation by
preschool children: the recognition of visual and haptic
stimuli presented separately and together, 'Journal of
Experimental Child Psychology', 12, 88-94.

MONTESSORI, M. (1915). 'The Montessori Method',
Heinemann, London.

MORGAN, W. PRINGLE (1896). A case of congenital word
blindness, 'British Medical Journal', 2, 1378.

MORRIS, J.M. (1966). 'Standards and Progress in Reading', NFER, Slough.

MUEHL, S. and KREMENAK, S. (1966). Ability to match
auditory and visual information within and between modalities and subsequent reading achievement, 'Journal of
Educational Psychology', 62, 482-6.

NAIDOO, S. (1972). 'Specific Dyslexia', Pitman, London.

NEISSER, U. (1967). 'Cognitive Psychology', Appleton-
Century-Crofts, New York.

NELSON, H.E. and WARRINGTON, E.K. (1974). Developmental spelling retardation and its relation to other cognitive abilities, 'British Journal of Psychology', 65, 265-
74.

NISBET, J.D. (1953). Family environment and intelligence, 'Eugenics Review', 45, 31-40.

NISBET, J.D. and ENTWISTLE, N.J. (1967). Intelligence and family size, 1949-1965, 'British Journal of
Educational Psychology', 37, 188-93.

NOELKER, R.W. and SCHUMSKY, D.A. (1973). Memory
for sequence, form and position as related to the identification of reading retardates, 'Journal of Educational
Psychology', 64, 22-5.

O'CONNOR, N. and HERMELIN, B.M. (1973). The spatial

or temporal organisation of short term memory, 'Quarterly Journal of Experimental Psychology', 25, 335-43.

OFMAN, W. and SHAEVITZ, M. (1963). The kinaesthetic method in remedial reading, 'Journal of Experimental Education', 31, 317-20.

O'NEILL, G. and STANLEY, G. (1976). Visual processing of straight lines in dyslexic and normal children, 'British Journal of Educational Psychology', 46, 323-7.

ORTON, S.T. (1928). Specific reading disability - strephosymbolia, 'Journal of the American Medical Association', 90, 1095-9.

ORTON, S.T. (1937). 'Reading, Writing and Speech Problems in Children', Chapman & Hall, London.

PAIVIO, A. (1971). 'Imagery and Verbal Processes', Holt, Rinehart & Winston, New York.

PAIVIO, A. (1975). Perceptual comparisons through the mind's eye, 'Memory and Cognition', 3, 635-47.

PAIVIO, A. and YARMEY, A.D. (1966). Pictures versus words as stimuli and responses in paired associate learning, 'Psychonomic Science', 5, 235-6.

PAIVIO, A., YUILLE, J. and MADIGAN, S. (1968). Concreteness imagery and meaningfulness for 925 nouns, 'Journal of Experimental Psychology', 76 (1 Part 2).

PARKS, T.E. and KROLL, N.E.A. (1975). Enduring visual memory despite forced verbal rehearsal, 'Journal of Experimental Psychology: Human Learning and Memory', 1, 648-54.

PARKS, T.E., KROLL, N.E.A., SALZBERG, P.M. and PARKINSON, S.R. (1972). Persistence of visual memory as indicated by decision time in a matching task, 'Journal of Experimental Psychology', 92, 437-8.

PATTERSON, K.E. and MARCEL, A.J. (1977). Aphasia, dyslexia and the phonological coding of written words, 'Quarterly Journal of Experimental Psychology', 29, 307-18.

PHILLIPS, W.A. (1974). On the distinction between sensory storage and short term visual memory, 'Perception and Psychophysics', 16, 283-90.

PHILLIPS, W.A. and BADDELEY, A.D. (1971). Reaction time and short term visual memory, 'Psychonomic Science', 22, 73-4.

POLLACK, R.H., PTASHNE, R.I. and CARTER, D.J. (1969). The effects of age and intelligence on the dark-interval threshold, 'Perception and Psychophysics', 6, 50-2.

POSNER, M.I. and KEELE, S.W. (1967). Decay of visual information from a single letter, 'Science', 158, 137-9.

PRINGLE, M.K., BUTLER, N. and DAVIE, R. (1966). '11,000 Seven-Year Olds', Longmans, London.

PULLIAM, R.A. (1945). Indented word-cards as a sensori-motor aid in vocabulary development, 'Peabody Journal of Education', 23, 38-42.

RICHARDSON, J.T.E. (1975a). The effect of word image-ability in acquired dyslexia, 'Neuropsychologia', 13, 281-8.

RICHARDSON, J.T.E. (1975b). Further evidence on the effect of word imageability in dyslexia, 'Quarterly Journal of Experimental Psychology', 27, 445-9.

ROBERTS, R.W. and COLEMAN, J.C. (1958). An investigation of the role of visual and kinaesthetic factors in reading failure, 'Journal of Educational Research', 51, 445-51.

ROBINSON, M.E. and SCHWARTZ, L.B. (1973). Visuo-motor skills and reading ability: a longitudinal study, 'Developmental Medicine and Child Neurology', 15, 281-6.

RUBENSTEIN, H., LEWIS, S. and RUBENSTEIN, M. A. (1971). Evidence for phonemic recoding in visual word recognition, 'Journal of Verbal Learning and Verbal Behavior', 10, 645-57.

RUDEL, R.G. and DENCKLA, M.B. (1974). Relation of forward and backward digit repetition to neurological impairment in children with learning disabilities, 'Neuro-psychologia', 12, 109-18.

RUDEL, R.G., DENCKLA, M.B. and SPALTEN, E. (1976). Paired associate learning of Morse code and Braille letter names by dyslexic and normal children, 'Cortex', 12, 61-70.

RUTTER, M. (1969). The concept of dyslexia, in P.H. Wolf and R. MacKeith (eds), 'Clinics in Developmental Medicine No 33, Planning for Better Learning', Spastics International Medical Publications, in association with Heinemann Medical Books, London.

RUTTER, M., TIZARD, J. and WHITMORE, K. (eds) (1970). 'Education, Health and Behaviour', Longmans, London.

RUTTER, M. and YULE, W. (1973). Specific reading retardation, in L. Mann and D. Sabatino (eds), 'The First Review of Special Education', Buttonwoods Farms, Philadelphia.

RUTTER, M. and YULE, W. (1975). The concept of specific reading retardation, 'Journal of Child Psychology and Psychiatry', 16, 181-97.

RUTTER, M., YULE, B., QUINTON, D., ROWLANDS, O., YULE, W. and BERGER, M. (1975). Attainment and adjustment in two geographical areas: III Some factors accounting for area differences, 'British Journal of Psychiatry', 126, 520-33.

SAFFRAN, E.M. and MARIN, O.S.M. (1977). Reading without phonology: evidence from aphasia, 'Quarterly Journal of Experimental Psychology', 29, 515-25.

SALZBERG, P.M., PARKS, T.E., KROLL, N.E.A. and PARKINSON, S.R. (1971). Retroactive effects of phonemic similarity on short-term recall of visual and auditory stimuli, 'Journal of Experimental Psychology', 91, 43-6.

SASANUMA, S. (1974). Kanji versus kana processing in alexia with transient agraphia: a case report, 'Cortex', 10, 89-97.

SATZ, P., RARDIN, D. and ROSS, J. (1971). An evaluation of a theory of specific developmental dyslexia, 'Child Development', 42, 2009-21.

SAVIN, H.B. (1972). What the child knows about speech when he starts to learn to read, in J.F. Mattingley and I.G. Kavanagh (eds), 'Language by Ear and by Eye: The Relationships Between Speech and Reading', MIT Press, Cambridge, Mass.

SAVIN, H.B. and BEVER, L.G. (1970). The nonperceptual reality of the phoneme, 'Journal of Verbal Learning and Verbal Behavior', 9, 295-302.

SHALLICE, T. and WARRINGTON, E.K. (1975). Word recognition in a phonemic dyslexic patient, 'Quarterly Journal of Experimental Psychology', 27, 187-99.

SHANKWEILER, D. and LIBERMAN, I.Y. (1976). Exploring the relations between reading and speech, in R.M. Knights and D.J. Bakker (eds), 'The Neuropsychology of Learning Disorders: Theoretical Approaches', University Parks Press, Baltimore.

SPERLING, G. (1960). The information available in brief visual presentations, 'Psychological Monographs', 74, no. 11.

SPRING, C. and CAPPS, C. (1974). Encoding speed, rehearsal, and probed recall of dyslexic boys, 'Journal of Educational Psychology', 66, 780-6.

STAMBAK, M. (1951). Le problème du rhythme dans le développement de l'enfant et dans les dyslexies d'évolution, 'Enfance', 5, 480-93.

STANLEY, G. (1975). Two-part stimulus integration and

specific reading disability, 'Perceptual and Motor Skills', 41, 873-4.

STANLEY, G. (1976). The processing of digits by children with specific reading disability (dyslexia), 'British Journal of Educational Psychology', 46, 81-4.

STANLEY, G. and HALL, R. (1973). Short-term visual information processing in dyslexics, 'Child Development', 44, 841-4.

STANLEY, G., KAPLAN, I. and POOLE, C. (1975). Cognitive and non-verbal perceptual processing in dyslexics, 'Journal of General Psychology', 93, 67-72.

STEGER, J.A., VELLUTINO, F.R. and MESHOULAM, U. (1972). Visual-tactile and tactile-tactile paired associate learning in normal and poor readers, 'Perceptual and Motor Skills', 35, 263-6.

STEVENSON, H.W. and MCBEE, G. (1958). The learning of object and pattern discriminations by children, 'Journal of Comparative and Physiological Psychology', 51, 752-4.

SUPRAMANIAM, S. and AUDLEY, R.J. (1976). The role of naming difficulties in reading backwardness, paper presented at the British Association annual conference, September.

SYMMES, J.S. and RAPOPORT, J.L. (1972). Unexpected reading failure, 'American Journal of Orthopsychiatry', 42, 82-91.

TALLAL, P. (1976). Auditory perceptual factors in language and learning disabilities, in R.M. Knights and D.J. Bakker (eds), 'The Neuropsychology of Learning Disorders', University Parks Press, Baltimore.

TALLAL, P. and PIERCY, M. (1973a). Defects of non-verbal auditory perception in children with developmental aphasia, 'Nature', 241, 468-9.

TALLAL, P. and PIERCY, M. (1973b). Developmental aphasia: impaired rate of non-verbal processing as a function of sensory modality, 'Neuropsychologia', 11, 389-98.

TALLAL, P. and PIERCY, M. (1974). Developmental aphasia: rate of auditory processing and selective impairment of consonant perception, 'Neuropsychologia', 12, 83-94.

TALLAL, P. and PIERCY, M. (1975). Developmental aphasia: the perception of brief vowels and extended stop consonants, 'Neuropsychologia', 13, 69-74.

TALMADGE, M., DAVIDS, A. and LAUFER, M.W. (1963). A study of experimental methods for teaching emotionally disturbed, brain–damaged retarded readers, 'Journal of Educational Research', 56, 311-16.

THOMAS, C.J. (1905). Congenital 'word blindness' and its treatment, 'Opthalmoscope', 3, 380-5.

THOR, D.H. and HOLDEN, E.A. (1969). Visual perception of sequential numerosity by normals and retardates, 'Journal of Abnormal Psychology', 74, 676-81.

TORDRUP, S.A. (1966). Reversals in reading and spelling, 'The Slow Learning Child', 12, 173-83.

TRABASSO, T. and BOWER, G.H. (1968). 'Attention in Learning: Theory and Research', Wiley, New York.

VANDE VOORT, L., SENF, G.M. and BENTON, A. (1972). Development of auditory–visual integration in normal and retarded readers, 'Child Development', 43, 1260-72.

VELLUTINO, F.R., BENTLEY, W.L. and PHILLIPS, F. (1978). Inter- versus intra–hemispheric learning in dyslexic and normal readers, 'Developmental Medicine and Child Neurology', 20, 71-80.

VELLUTINO, F.R., DESETTO, L. and STEGER, J.A. (1972). Categorical judgement and the Wepman test of auditory discrimination, 'Journal of Speech and Hearing Disorders', 37, 252-7.

VELLUTINO, F.R., HARDING, C.J., PHILLIPS, F. and STEGER, J.A. (1975). Differential transfer in poor and normal readers, 'Journal of Genetic Psychology', 126, 3-18.

VELLUTINO, F.R., PRUZEK, R.M., STEGER, J.A. and MESHOULHAM, U. (1973). Immediate visual recall in poor and normal readers as a function of orthographic-linguistic familiarity, 'Cortex', 9, 368-84.

VELLUTINO, F.R., STEGER, J.A., DESETTO, L. and PHILLIPS, F. (1975). Immediate and delayed recognition of visual stimuli in poor and normal readers, 'Journal of Experimental Child Psychology', 19, 223-32.

VELLUTINO, F.R., STEGER, J.A., HARDING, C.J. and PHILLIPS, F. (1975). Verbal vs. non–verbal paired associates learning in poor and normal readers, 'Neuropsychologia', 13, 75-82.

VELLUTINO, F.R., STEGER, J.A., KAMAN, M. and DESETTO, L. (1975). Visual form perception in deficient and normal readers as a function of age and orthographic linguistic familiarity, 'Cortex', 11, 22-30.

VELLUTINO, F.R., STEGER, J.A. and KANDEL, G. (1972). Reading disability: an investigation of the perceptual deficit hypothesis, 'Cortex', 8, 106-18.

VELLUTINO, F.R., STEGER, J.A. and PRUZEK, R.M. (1973). Inter vs intra-sensory deficit in paired associate learning in poor and normal readers, 'Canadian Journal of Behavioral Science', 5, 111-23.

VERNON, M.D. (1970). Specific developmental dyslexia, in A.W. Franklin and S. Naidoo (eds), 'Assessment and Teaching of Dyslexic Children', Invalid Children's Aid Association, London.

WALTERS, R.H. and DOAN, H. (1962). Perceptual and cognitive functioning of retarded readers, 'Journal of Consulting Psychology', 26, 355-61.

WARREN, R.M. (1970). Perceptual restoration of missing speech sounds, 'Science', 167, 392-3.

WARREN, R.M. (1971). Identification times for phonemic components of graded complexity and for spelling of speech, 'Perception and Psychophysics', 9, 345-9.

WARREN, R.M. (1976). Auditory perception and speech evolution, 'Annals of the New York Academy of Sciences', 280, 708-17.

WARREN, R.M. and OBUSEK, C.J. (1971). Speech perception and phonemic restorations, 'Perception and Psychophysics', 9, 358-62.

WARREN, R.M. and SHERMAN, G.I. (1974). Phonemic restorations based on subsequent context, 'Perception and Psychophysics', 16, 150-6.

WECHSLER, D. and HAGIN, R.A. (1964). The problem of axial rotation in reading disability, 'Perceptual and Motor Skills', 19, 319-26.

WEINER, B. and GOODNOW, J.J. (1970). Motor activity: effects on memory, 'Developmental Psychology', 2, 448.

WEISS, W. and MARGOLIUS, G. (1954). The effect of context stimuli on learning and retention, 'Journal of Experimental Psychology', 48, 318-22.

WEPMAN, J.M. (1958). 'The Auditory Discrimination Test', Language Research Associates, Chicago.

WHIPPLE, C.I. and KODMAN, F. (1969). A study of discrimination and perceptual learning with retarded readers, 'Journal of Educational Psychology', 60, 1-5.

WICKER, F.W. (1970). On the locus of picture-word differences in paired associate learning, 'Journal of Verbal Learning and Verbal Behavior', 9, 52-7.

WILLIAMS, H.L., BEAVER, W.S., SPENCE, M.T. and RUNDELL, O.H. (1969). Digital and kinaesthetic memory with interpolated information processing, 'Journal of Experimental Psychology', 80, 530-6.

WILLIAMS, J. (1975). Training children to copy and to discriminate letter like forms, 'Journal of Educational Psychology', 67, 790-5.

WOLFF, A.G. (1970). The Gillingham-Stillman programme, in A.W. Franklin and S. Naidoo (eds), 'Assessment and Teaching of Dyslexic Children', Invalid Children's Aid Association, London.

YULE, W. (1973). Differential prognosis of reading backwardness and specific reading retardation, 'British Journal of Educational Psychology', 43, 244-8.

YULE, W. (1976). Issues and problems in remedial education, 'Developmental Medicine and Child Neurology', 18, 675-82.

YULE, W., RUTTER, M., BERGER, M. and THOMPSON, J. (1974). Over- and under-achievement in reading: distribution in the general population, 'British Journal of Educational Psychology', 44, 1-12.

ZUNG, B.J., BUTTER, E.J. and CASHDAN, S. (1974). Visual-haptic form recognition with task delay and sequenced bimodal input, 'Neuropsychologia', 12, 73-81.

ZURIF, E.B. and CARSON, G. (1970). Dyslexia in relation to cerebral dominance and temporal analysis, 'Neuropsychologia', 8, 351-61.

# Subject index

# Name index